In 1974, sitting in his off
Sydney, John Marsden n
advertisement for a teaching course. Bored and frustrated by his job, John applied for the course, was
accepted, and began teaching in 1978. In his first year
he taught P.E., Remedial Reading, and curated the
First XI cricket pitch. Just as the year started he was
also given an English class of feral Year 10s, who put
him through a gruelling survival course in classroom
management.

John survived, and by 1984 he was Head of English
at Geelong Grammar's famous Timbertop campus.
Three years later John's first novel was published. *So
Much to Tell You* became one of Australia's most successful books and a string of international hits
followed, including *The Other Side of Dawn* which was a
number one bestseller.

John Marsden now lives at the Tye Estate, just outside of Melbourne, where he takes writing courses for
young people and adults. His next novel, *Winter*, will
be published in 2000.

Also by John Marsden

So Much to Tell You
The Journey
The Great Gatenby
Staying Alive in Year 5
Out of Time
Letters from the Inside
Take My Word for It
Looking for Trouble
Tomorrow . . . (Ed.)
Cool School
Creep Street
Checkers
For Weddings and a Funeral (Ed.)
This I Believe (Ed.)
Dear Miffy
Prayer for the Twenty-First Century
Everything I Know About Writing
Secret Men's Business
The Rabbits
Norton's Hut

The *Tomorrow* Series

Tomorrow, When the War Began
The Dead of the Night
The Third Day, the Frost
Darkness, Be My Friend
Burning for Revenge
The Night is for Hunting
The Other Side of Dawn

MARSDEN ON MARSDEN

THE STORIES BEHIND JOHN MARSDEN'S BESTSELLING BOOKS

John Marsden

PAN
Pan Macmillan Australia

Extracts from the Australian edition of *So Much to Tell You*
by John Marsden, published by Thomas C. Lothian Pty Ltd,
reproduced with permission.

All reasonable attempts have been made to obtain permission to quote
from material. If any have been inadvertently omitted, the publishers
will be pleased to make corrections at the earliest opportunity.

John Marsden's website can be visited at:
http://www.macmillan.com.au/pma/marsden

First published 2000 in Pan by Pan Macmillan Australia Pty Limited
St Martins Tower, 31 Market Street, Sydney

National Library of Australia
cataloguing-in-publication data:

Marsden, John, 1950– .
Marsden on Marsden: the stories behind
John Marsden's bestselling books.

ISBN 0 330 36216 X.

1. Marsden, John, 1950– – Influences.
2. Young adult fiction, Australian.
3. Authors, Australian – 20th century. I. Title.

A828.303

Cover images (top row, l–r): Digital Stock, Katie Morgan
(middle row, l–r): Digital Stock, Maikka Trupp, Digital Stock
(bottom row, l–r): Vivienne Goodman, Andrew Craig Steinman

Typeset in 11/13 pt New Baskerville by Post Pre-press Group
Printed in Australia by McPherson's Printing Group

For James 'Rob Roy' Fraser, who gave life to most of my books, and, somewhere along the way, became a good friend.

CONTENTS

Chapter One
So Much to Tell You   1

Chapter Two
Take My Word for It   21

Chapter Three
The Great Gatenby   28

Chapter Four
The Journey   36

Chapter Five
Out of Time   45

Chapter Six
Letters from the Inside   52

Chapter Seven
Tomorrow, When the War Began   66

Chapter Eight
The Sequels to *Tomorrow, When the War Began*   81

Chapter Nine
Checkers   103

Chapter Ten
Dear Miffy   110

Chapter Eleven
Winter   118

A Final Word   123

Chapter One

So Much to Tell You

When I was nineteen I met a girl who didn't speak. She was a patient in a psychiatric hospital in Sydney.

So was I. Feeling depressed and suicidal, I had been admitted to the hospital in an attempt to resolve some of the problems in my life.

I don't know much about the girl, but I'll call her Rachel. She was fourteen and hadn't spoken for eight months. The gossip around the hospital was that her parents had separated, and Rachel was living with her father and stepmother. She didn't like her stepmother, and had gradually become more withdrawn and depressed, until she shut down completely.

In the ward she made no eye contact with anybody. She moved by pressing into a wall and shuffling along sideways. The rest of the time she stayed huddled in a corner. I was horrified and saddened to see someone so isolated, so unhappy.

One morning I was in the dining area, getting my

breakfast on a tray before taking it to a table. A man in the queue began talking to me about Rachel: 'Did you realise she's going home today?'

'No, I didn't. How come she's going home? Is she talking now?'

'Yes,' he said. 'She's been talking for a few weeks.'

We decided to have breakfast with her. We took our trays to her table and started a conversation. She was still very shy but she was talking, and she was excited and pleased to be going home. It was wonderful to see the improvement in her condition.

I never saw her again. Eventually the time came for me to leave the hospital too. But I often wondered about Rachel. Was she happy? Was she still talking? What was her real story?

Some years later I found myself teaching at All Saints' College, a small private school in Bathurst, New South Wales. All my life I'd had the urge to write, and during my time in Bathurst I made yet another attempt to put something on paper. This time it was a film script. John Mazur, a Canadian who taught English at the school, had been an inspiration to me and had profoundly affected my life, showing me how much a teacher can achieve, how creative a teacher can be, and how the best teachers take risks by exploring the curriculum in adventurous ways.

John was particularly effective with students who had emotional problems. I started wondering what might have happened had Rachel come into contact with John Mazur – if Rachel had been a student at the school perhaps. So one holiday I started writing a script using that scenario. With a teacher's disintegrating marriage providing a subplot, the script told the story of a deeply troubled girl who comes to a small boarding school, where the teacher helps her regain a sense of identity and a voice.

> *LINDELL (at staff meeting): I think we should*
> *hang in there a little longer with her. I can't exactly*
> *give you a reason – at least not one that's going to*
> *make sense. I just think there's something*
> *happening there and if we give her a little more*
> *time ... I mean she's not going to leap up from her*
> *desk and start talking, just because Max here*
> *touches her with the sacred blackboard duster ...*
> *Maybe the talking's not the main thing anyway.*
> *PRINCIPAL: What do you mean?*
> *LINDELL: Well, what's so great about talking? I*
> *mean, there's plenty of days I don't talk to anyone*
> *and you don't send me off to an institution.*
> *MAX: Don't count on that.*
> *LINDELL: Well, I think the main thing for*
> *Marina is trust ...*

I sent the script to a couple of film companies and the ABC. One film company didn't reply, another wrote to say they had dropped out of the production business, but an ABC producer sent me a thoughtful and generous letter with extensive comments on my work.

I was impressed and touched by his reaction, even though the bottom line was that he still rejected the project. But years later I was reminded of that letter when I read in the preface to Emily Brontë's *Wuthering Heights* of the effect of a kind word on Charlotte. Brontë described how she was encouraged by a Scottish publisher: 'I ventured to apply to the Messrs Chambers, of

Edinburgh, for a word of advice; they may have forgotten the circumstance, but I have not, for from them I received a brief and business-like, but civil and sensible reply, on which we acted and at last made a way.'

The essentials of this film script were later to become the main elements of *So Much to Tell You*, but there were many differences. In the script the teacher played a bigger role, and his professional and personal life formed a larger part of the material. Jane – the character who became Sophie in the book – was explored more fully in the film script, and she too underwent a transformation, intended to mirror Marina's.

However, when the script was rejected I did not think much about these characters or situations again for quite a while. Until 1986, in fact. By then I was teaching at Geelong Grammar's Timbertop School, a bush campus between Mansfield and Mt Buller, where Year 9 students spend their full academic year. Timbertop is an unusual and challenging experience. Not only do the students have little contact with their families, but they undertake a physically and mentally demanding programme, including long-distance runs of up to 28 kilometres, cross-country ski trips camping in the snow, and hikes of up to six days, carrying their supplies on their backs.

For four years I taught at Timbertop, enjoying much of it, but still feeling dissatisfied with my life. One day I was reading a book called *The Uses of the Imagination*, by Bruno Bettleheim, in which Bettleheim analyses the hidden meaning of fairy stories like 'Little Red Riding Hood' and 'Jack and the Beanstalk'. Bettleheim claims, for example, that Jack's three trips up the beanstalk are symbolic of the three stages of life. The first trip, on which he brings back the bag of gold, represents the childish desire to have a lucky win, to achieve everything you want through magic. Many adults – especially people who gamble a lot – are still at this stage. The second trip up the beanstalk, from which Jack returns with the golden goose which lays the gold eggs, represents a more mature attitude: where you realise that one lucky strike isn't enough; you need a regular income, a steady job. On Jack's third trip he brings back the golden harp, and Bettleheim explains that this symbolises true maturity. Jack realises that money and work are not everything. The mature person appreciates music, art, theatre, literature.

I was embarrassed when reading this analysis to realise that, although I didn't hang out at the casino or TAB, in some ways I was still at the first stage. But Bettleheim's book made me understand that if I wanted to achieve my goals, to make my dreams come true, I would have to do some work. It wouldn't just happen automatically.

I sat down and asked myself two questions: 'What do I want to achieve?' and 'What do I think is my greatest strength?'

The answer to both questions was pretty much the same: I wanted to become an author, and I thought writing was my best skill.

As it happened, a journalist and photographer from *Woman's Day* had recently visited the school. Unbeknown to me, some students showed the photographer an article I had written for the school magazine. They told me how the photographer read it, then said to the students: 'This guy's in the wrong job. He should be writing.'

That comment came at the right moment. I resolved to have a serious go at becoming an author.

I made a few decisions that turned out to be crucial. I'd noticed that my Year 9 students weren't reading – or if they did read they chose shallow and melodramatic books like *Flowers in the Attic*. So I decided to try writing for that age group. I was also aware that something was wrong with my approach to writing, because every time I sat down to write a novel, I got twenty or thirty pages into it but then ran out of steam. The film script I worked on in Bathurst and a very bad novel that I wrote when I was twenty were all that I'd finished, in fifteen years of trying.

I analysed why I couldn't finish anything, and decided it was because I spent too much time editing. Typically I'd write a couple of pages, then the next day sit down and edit, re-edit and polish everything I'd done the day before. A few hours of this would drain my creative energy and I then couldn't be bothered writing much more of the book. After a few weeks I'd give up completely.

So I decided that this time I would write an entire book in the three-week school vacation. I didn't care how short it was. I also decided that, no matter how strong the temptation, I wouldn't do any editing until the book was finished.

The holidays started. I was staying at a friend's house in Torquay. She had gone to London on impulse and left me to look after the house. I started writing, using the same story that still held such fascination for me, that of 'Rachel' and the imagined encounter with John Mazur. The words poured out. Each day I wanted to go back to the beginning and read what I'd done but I didn't give in. I allowed myself to read the most recent paragraph or two, so I could get back in the mood of the story, but that was the only concession I made.

I finished the book in the three weeks.

It was quite a powerful moment when I sat down to read my own novel for the first time. Because I had been so emotionally involved in writing it, I couldn't remember many of the scenes, so it was like reading a book by someone else. There were times when I genuinely didn't know what would happen next.

I thought the novel had something. It was short but there seemed to be an emotional intensity that I could feel, even though it was my own work.

When I went back to school I gave the manuscript to three students and asked them to tell me what they thought. Well, they weren't stupid; they all wanted A's for English and they knew how to keep their teacher happy. But their responses did impress me as more than just courteous or obsequious. One girl, Samantha, told me how she wept as she read the book. I thought, 'There must be something working here.'

I sent the manuscript to six different publishers, just names I'd pulled out of the Yellow Pages. Within a short time the rejections began to arrive, and soon I had the full set of six. It was quite discouraging and I thought sadly: 'Well, obviously I was wrong about the book.' I put it in the bottom drawer of the desk (literally), and went back to teaching English.

A few months later Albert Ullin, a Melbourne bookseller, rang me. A New Zealand writer was in Victoria and was available to speak to school students. Would it be all right if he brought her to Timbertop?

'Sure,' I replied. 'What's her name?'

'Margaret Mahy,' he said.

The name meant little to me but I was happy for her to visit, and I reminded myself to check out her books before she came. Unfortunately I didn't have time to do that but I sat in the back of the chapel and listened enthralled, as this lively and sparky lady gave a terrific address to the students. That night I went out to dinner with Albert, Margaret, and a publisher's representative. Brashly, during the meal, I told them that I too had written a book, and sent it to six different publishers, but all had rejected it.

The publisher was horrified. 'You don't do it that way!' she exclaimed. 'You don't send it to more than one publisher at a time.'

'Why not?' I asked.

'You just don't,' she said firmly. 'That's not the way the industry works.'

I could see how it was in the best interest of publishers for an author to send his manuscript to one publisher at a time. It put that publisher in a powerful position, where if they made an offer to an author, no matter how small, the author would be tempted to accept. After all, if you refuse, what do you do then? Hope you can find another publisher who likes you? That might take years, or might never happen. When I'd sent my book to six different publishers, I'd fondly imagined a bidding war where they would compete fiercely, with open chequebooks, for the right to the manuscript.

I think Albert must have gotten sick of the conversation, because he brought it to an end by offering to read my manuscript and advise me on what to do with it.

I accepted gratefully.

The next day I started reading some of Margaret Mahy's books and was as inspired by them as I was mortified by my ignorance of her reputation. I was embarrassed to think that I had mentioned my measly little story in front of someone who had won a Carnegie Medal. I was also disappointed that I had been dining with someone of such extraordinary intellect and imagination and I hadn't taken advantage of the opportunity by getting her to talk more about her life and work.

Nevertheless, I did take up Albert's invitation and I sent him the manuscript. I heard nothing for some time so after a few months I rang him.

'Yes,' he said, 'I have read it and I've just given it to a friend of mine who is starting a publishing company; a guy named Walter McVitty.'

I had read a newspaper article about McVitty's venture into publishing so I recognised the name.

More time passed and I heard nothing from McVitty. Eventually I rang him and introduced myself over the phone.

'Yes,' he said, 'I do have your book. It's on my pile of manuscripts, and getting closer to the top, so I should be reading it in the next few weeks.'

A month or two later I had a letter from him in which he expressed a tentative willingness to publish the book if I did more editorial work.

Filled with excitement and optimism, I went around telling everybody that I was having a book published. This was really quite a leap from the cautiousness of McVitty's letter, but I was confident I could do the editorial work required. So next holidays I sat down and resumed work. I made the book longer, by about fifty per cent, and changed the opening and ending. It originally ended with this passage:

> *So, this is where I am, on this night, May 25,*
> *eleven days from my fifteenth birthday, sitting in*
> *the Prep Room of Year 9 Dorm B at Warrington.*
> *And this is where I wanted to be. Today was a*
> *ratty day. Tomorrow could be the same or worse, or*
> *it could be better. Whatever, it is my decision, and*
> *I can live with it. It feels good. It feels right for me.*
> *It's a long way from the sleep to the dream. But*
> *I'm still in with a chance. It's like Mr Lindell said*
> *in class today: 'The darker the night, the brighter*
> *burns the candle.'*

To me, this seemed a good place to stop, as it was obvious that Marina was going to be OK. She was taking charge of her own life again, and that was all the reader needed to know. But I was happy with the new ending too.

I also added some more humour, as McVitty had suggested. Then I sent it off again. This time his response was more positive, and he made a definite offer to publish.

At this stage the novel's working title was *Diary*, hardly imaginative, but I've always liked understatement and I thought something so plain and simple would be a refreshing change from the over-clever titles many books seemed to be using. To be honest though I never expected a publisher to like that name. When, after further editing, I got the ending right, McVitty suggested we use the last sentence as a title and I agreed it was likely to work better.

Like most authors I was upset by any suggestions from McVitty that involved changing a single word of the book, but I have to admit that his editing improved the manuscript a lot. The only argument we had was over swearing. In the original text Marina swore half a dozen times. McVitty warned against that, saying that the book didn't need it and it wasn't good to be controversial. In a letter to me, he wrote: 'I'm well aware that people swear, but I'd prefer they didn't in our books.' ('Our', meaning books published by Walter and his wife.)

Finally, in some irritation I said to him over the phone: 'All right, take the swear words out then.'

I probably said, 'All right, take the bloody swear words out.' Or worse.

I hadn't realised that, instead of removing them, McVitty would put new words in their place. I was horrified when I got a copy of the the book to find that he had substituted the word 'damned', a word which no teenager would use in that context and a word that was entirely wrong for Marina. By the time I realised, it was too late for me to do anything; the book was published. It's highly unusual for a publisher to change words in a book without discussing it with the author and it wasn't a good development in our relationship.

There were a few early positive signs for *So Much to Tell You*. McVitty told me that his son, who didn't like reading, read it in one sitting and became quite fulsome in expressing his praise for it. My brother wrote me a very moving letter saying how much the book had affected him and predicting success for it. Again it seemed more than conventional courtesy or family loyalty. It was a passionate and heartfelt response.

I came across a copy of the *Sydney Morning Herald* by chance, in which a review of recommended new children's books contained a couple of paragraphs about *So Much to Tell You.* Then there was a phone call from my parents saying that the book was number nine on a list of bestsellers from a children's bookshop in Melbourne. Then there was a visit to Shearer's Bookshop in Gordon, where I asked for suggestions of good recent releases for young readers.

'Hardcover or paperback?' the sales assistant asked.

'Paperback,' I said firmly, not wanting to face the embarrassment of having my own book, which was in hardcover, either recommended or ignored.

The young woman picked out half a dozen titles then suddenly said, 'I know you said paperback, but there is a new hardcover which has just come in and which we all love. Everybody's raving about it.'

She picked *So Much to Tell You* off the shelf and held it out to me.

I wished the floor would open up and swallow me. I knew I was going a deep red. I had already agreed to buy the books she'd shown me and I had to pay by credit card, so even if I said nothing she would see my name. I had no choice but to blurt out: 'I wrote it.'

Her reaction was as exciting as it was embarrassing. Within a couple of minutes the whole sales staff had gathered and I was answering questions from them as well as from a couple of customers. And although I felt uncomfortable at the time, for years afterwards the incident gave me a warm glow whenever I thought about it.

After that things happened pretty quickly. *So Much to Tell You* was shortlisted for the Australian Children's Book Council Book of the Year Award, which genuinely astonished me. I thought this award was reserved for writers who had been around for decades and were institutions in the book world – people like Nan Chauncy, Ivan Southall, Colin Thiele, Joan Phipson, Patricia Wrightson. But when I read the other books shortlisted I thought I had a chance. A couple of them were fantastic, but a couple of them were pretty weak, and I felt that at least *So Much to Tell You* wasn't disgraced by being in their company. It was actually a bigger shock for me to be shortlisted than it was to win.

By then I was working at Geelong Grammar's main campus, Corio. I had no telephone of my own, but about half past ten one morning the phone in the duty area rang. I picked it up, identified myself, and heard Walter McVitty's voice saying: 'Open the champagne.'

The next few weeks rushed past. There were huge numbers of messages of congratulation, from family, friends, past and present students. I had to make sudden arrangements to go to Perth to accept the prize. Sales of the book went through the roof and I found myself giving media interviews. It was a very exciting time.

I was amused to realise that the students at Timbertop who loyally bought a copy of the book when it first appeared – some of them more enthusiastically than others – had actually made a good investment. Only 2,000 copies were printed in the book's first edition. Over the years they have steadily appreciated in value and are now worth at least five times what the students paid for them in 1987.

My author copies of *So Much to Tell You* did not arrive until after the book was published, and as I had not seen any designs, drawings or drafts for the cover, I didn't have much idea of what to expect. Nevertheless, handling the first copies of the book had been a precious and exciting moment, and one that still makes me smile when I recall it.

Years later McVitty reacted very bitterly to my decision to give *Take My Word for It* to another publisher but I am grateful to him for giving me the chance to get published, and I am grateful for much of his editing. I think he was right about deleting the swear words, but I smiled at the irony years later when he published a new edition of *Seven Little Australians*. He said: '. . . I have reinstated Pip's "My oath!" (in Chapter 11), which was modified for the second edition to "My word!" by the nervous publisher, in response to criticism that the former was tantamount to swearing.'

It made me wonder whether someone might do the same for *So Much to Tell You* one day, with a similar reference to the publisher of that book.

The first overseas country to publish the book was the USA, and it was quite an experience for me to deal with American publishers. They had an early problem with the word Milo. I got a phone call about three o'clock one morning, from the Boston editor, who obviously didn't realise we have a different time zone to them. Only half awake, I heard a voice saying: 'Excuse me, what is Milo? The girl in your book uses Milo. Is it some kind of drug you people have?'

'Yes,' I replied, 'It's a real problem here. Teenagers are sniffing Milo and shooting up on Milo all around the country. Only last week a girl down the road over-dosed on it . . .'

Eventually I had to tell them the truth. The next question was: 'Can we change it to Ovaltine or cocoa? We don't have Milo in this country.'

The major point that the American publishers kept reiterating to me was that Americans aren't subtle. Everything has to be spelt out for them. They can't read between the lines. I thought this was a surprising attitude for a publisher to have, especially given that a lot of the best American writers are very subtle indeed, and are immensely popular in their own country.

Nevertheless, I eventually agreed to write an extra section to the book, which would make the attack on Marina's face more explicit to American readers.

I wasn't sure about this, but I thought I would have a go, and if it didn't work I could always tell them that I had changed my mind about doing it. However, I was quite happy with the finished product. It is now included in the American edition of the book – the only overseas edition that contains this section. For the interest of Australian readers, it is reproduced here for the first time in this country.

JUNE 15

Today in English we did that scene from Our Town *where Emily gets the chance to relive a day from her childhood. She chose a happy day, her twelfth birthday. A happy day.*

I sat there gazing out the window, listening to Cathy's voice as she read Emily, and to Rikki's as

*she read the part of the Stage Manager. I remember
sitting in English a while back, thinking how I'd
like to see a replay of a day in my life. Only one
day, in a lifetime of days. In fact, not even the
whole day – just a few minutes.*

*Mr Lindell said: 'If you added up all the
really significant episodes in your life, they'd
probably come to less than sixty minutes.'*

*I could see the chapel in the rain, and a
willow tree beaded with drops of water, its branches
snaking around in the wind.*

*The whole thing only took five minutes, I'd
say. It was a fortnight after the Family Court
hearing. I'm still not too sure about the details. I
only ever saw one newspaper and that was by
accident, months later, at my grandmother's place.
It seems like it was just after my mother had been
awarded half his money when he found out about
his business, and how Mr Aird had milked all its
assets, at the same time as he was having an
affair with my mother. He found all that out in
one big hit.*

*That was what the paper said, but I think
there was more to it than that even.*

*The paper said my father was going to kill
Mr Aird, but what happened to me changed
everything. Hope Mr Aird's grateful. I never saw
him again. I don't know what happened to him.
Probably nothing.*

*Emily was told to pick a special day in her life.
She chose a happy day. I'd choose a day called
April 14, at seven o'clock. The ABC News was just
starting on the radio, as we drove up to the house.*

My mother got out at the steps. Oh, God, how I remember. She'd been lecturing me on how I was too shy. I had to get out and meet more people. Get some confidence in myself. I picked up her hat, which was next to me on the front seat, and put it on. 'Does this hat give you confidence?' I asked. I'm shaking like an old person, writing this. 'Can I put the car away?' She let me sometimes. 'Yes, be careful,' she said. Sort of automatically. I slid over to the driver's seat. It was a new car. Ah yes, of course – now I realise how she could afford it. I started the engine, then searched for the headlight switch. Nearly couldn't find it in the darkness, but then I did. Switched them on. High beam, but didn't matter. Drove around the corner, into the garage. Switched the lights off. My last moments as a person. Switched the engine off. Quiet in the garage. A ticking sound, as the car cooled down. Shadows, very large. A scuffling noise somewhere. A dark shape, suddenly moving. Oh no, imagination, surely? No, real. What? A human. An arm? Through the window. Attacking me? No, still safe for an instant. Still an instant of hope, of waiting, as fear starts growing. Then the arm moving so fast. With violence. Something thrown, wetting my face. Still that hope, that it mightn't be bad. A joke, maybe? Whoever it is will get into lots of trouble, and I'm glad. They deserve to. Then just screaming and pain. I remember that no scream was loud enough. Burning and grabbing and screaming, wanting to tear the skin from my face, tear my face off. But however loudly I screamed, it didn't make it any better. That wasn't

*fair. It took so long for anyone to come, anything
to happen. Less than sixty minutes, did Mr
Lindell say? But this took a lifetime, Mr Lindell.
No, a death time.*

*Everyone in the class staring at me. What
happened? What did I do? Did I make a noise?
For a long moment we're all locked into stares at
each other. Then they turn back to their books,
embarrassed. They will talk about it later.*

*Mr Lindell speaks to Lisa. 'It's your line, Mrs
Webb. Emily's father has a surprise for her. Line
twenty-four.'*

Not long before I started writing *So Much to Tell You*, a
Melbourne woman, a prostitute named Kay Nesbitt,
was shot in the head through the door of her apart-
ment. Her face was so terribly damaged that a
number of people working at the hospital where she
was admitted wondered whether they should be trying to save her. They thought she might be better off
dead. Some of them believed that Kay would kill herself anyway, when she saw her face. Months later, one
of the surgeons who operated on her was asked about
his comment that Kay might wish for death when she
realised the seriousness of the damage done to her.
He replied: 'Yes, well I think that turned out to be
bullshit . . . I grossly underestimated the woman and I
did that through a prejudiced and stupid attitude
because of her trade . . .' (Quoted in *Face Value* by Bill
Birnbauer, Penguin 1989).

I was inspired by this gutsy and spirited woman, and
her story wove itself into *So Much to Tell You*, without my
even planning it. 'Rachel' from the hospital in Sydney

and Kay Nesbitt combined to become Marina. The link I made in my mind as I wrote was based on the importance we attach to our faces: the way in which they are related to our feelings of self worth and identity.

In *So Much to Tell You* I wanted to explore a number of ideas. The most crucial of these is Marina's loss of identity, of which her silence is just one symptom. I wanted to establish this loss in more ways than that though. So, I gave her no name, no family (in any meaningful sense of the word), no friends, and a new face. By the end of the book, her success in finding a new identity for herself is signalled by changes in all those circumstances. She has connected with her father again, she is making friends, she is coming to terms with her new face, she starts to talk, and so she gets a name. It's like a baptism, of the new person.

For many people adolescence is something like that: a search for a new identity built on the realisation that one's identity as a child has started to dissolve. To have a good adult life, the search has to be successful.

Other themes that interested me were the power of creative individuals, and the power of friendship. The creative teaching and the personal sensitivity of Mr Lindell mirrored the real-life teaching of John Mazur. I had been able to witness first hand his inspiring effect on students, especially those who were damaged or at risk. Equally, I have seen the supportive loving friendships that many teenagers are lucky enough to experience, and how valuable they can be during dark times. I wanted to celebrate those things in the book.

The ending of *So Much to Tell You* annoyed a lot of people, but I stopped where I did because I thought readers knew everything they needed to know. Marina is clearly going to make it. She's reached the point where she'll take three steps forward for every two back.

So Much to Tell You was for many years the biggest-selling teenage novel ever published in Australia – until overtaken by *Tomorrow, When the War Began*. It has been published in eleven languages in fourteen countries. I have great affection for it, as the book that dramatically changed my life.

Chapter Two

Take My Word for It

Even though *Take My Word for It* was my seventh book, it seems appropriate to talk about it here, because of its relationship to *So Much to Tell You.*

By the time *Take My Word for It* came out, the most frequent question people were asking me was: 'Why do you always write from a girl's point of view?' It was a surprising question in one sense, because of my six novels to that date, four were written from the perspective of male characters. But the two most popular, *So Much to Tell You* and *Letters from the Inside,* had girls as the protagonists.

I do like writing about female characters. It's partly because I find females interesting and complex. I suspect that deep in all males is the knowledge that no matter how hard we try, we'll never understand women. Perhaps women feel the same way about men. Elusiveness can be very fascinating.

I think another reason I write from a female point

w is that, like many males, I have found it hard to develop an emotional voice. I was brought up in the 50s and 60s, when men weren't allowed to have feelings. Perhaps as a result, when I write emotional books I feel more comfortable doing so from a female perspective. It probably explains why, of my first seven books, the three most emotional ones have female protagonists.

For all that, however, *Take My Word for It* was not written in the state of emotional intensity that I felt when I wrote *So Much to Tell You* or *Letters from the Inside*. Those moods don't come very often. *Take My Word for It* was more a story I wanted to have the enjoyment of telling. It was born of my liking for the characters in the first book, my desire to write more about them, to get to know them better – in short, to revisit them. It came also from the obvious interest of readers in their lives.

Take My Word for It is full of big and little stories that I collected in my years of teaching at boarding schools. I didn't collect them cold-bloodedly, like a scientist picking up specimens; I only had to keep my eyes and ears open to soak up an amazing number of real-life experiences. The story of Lisa's father's wedding, for example, is more or less true. Perhaps in boarding schools you hear more stories. It certainly seemed that way to me.

I've always found it more interesting to write about strong characters than weak ones. Both Marina and Lisa are strong in their different ways, and of course they have a lot in common. I'm especially fascinated by 'strong silent types': people who internalise, who have intense feelings but can't find the words to express them.

In boarding schools I saw a lot of unhappy people, who, when they did talk, often had sad and horrifying stories to tell. I remember, for example, a boy asking me: 'Can your mother stop you from seeing your father?' He was caught in the middle of a ferocious battle between the two parents. I remember another boy asking me what people look like after they die. His questions got more and more specific, until at last he told me why he was asking: 'My father committed suicide and I've always wondered what he looked like when he was dead.' And I remember one boy telling me how when his mother left, she took everything in the house, all his toys, even his teddy.

I saw primary-school boarders arrive back for the new term with notes saying, 'We can't look after Lucy (or Jack or whoever) next holidays. Please find someone she (or he) can stay with . . .' I saw students from overseas come to school with thousands of dollars in cash and instructions to book themselves into a motel for the next holidays. I saw students distraught with grief when they found that their father wouldn't come on Visiting Day because their mother was going to be there.

So although this book was not written in a whitehot emotional state, nevertheless emotions like anger and sadness played their part. At the same time the book reflects my enjoyment of the more positive aspects of boarding-school life and my admiration of the gutsiness and good humour of the young people I taught, who often displayed great resilience in the face of appalling difficulties. Lisa is based loosely on a student I admired. Her personal life was complicated but her courage and determination were extreme.

She became well known for her physical and mental strength; qualities which saw her achieving staggering results in the tough hiking and running programme at Timbertop. In fact there was something worrying about her driven personality, as there is with Lisa in the book.

'You're as sick as your secrets,' Liza Minnelli is supposed to have said. Anything internalised is liable to do damage. The more controlled someone is on the outside, the more out of control they're likely to be on the inside. Conversely, talking to the right person can help enormously. These are some of the issues I wanted to explore in *Take My Word for It*, and they are some of the lessons Lisa has to learn.

For a book to be effective the central character has to change, evolve, grow. She has to learn something. Lisa does gradually and painfully make progress. One of the things she learns is to stop being so tough on herself.

Some of the scenes I most enjoyed writing are the ones which show the daily life of young people. I love the commonplace, the minutiae of human existence. Hence, the rowing scenes are among my favourites of anything I've ever written.

APRIL 16

Dearest Diary, this is what happened. The weather was beautiful, the water was smooth, the wind was down. We drew lane one, which everyone said was the fastest. With everything going so perfectly I knew I'd catch a crab and fall out of the boat in the first hundred metres. We got an OK start, not

*as good as University, but not too bad. They had a
length on us at the 600 and I was getting worried,
but we were long and strong, rating 28, and c, c
and c (cool, calm and collected). It was so different
from the Fourths, where by this stage Rebecca
would be screaming at Kate, I'd be screaming at
Rebecca, and Myra would be screaming at all of
us. But this time we did ten hard through the
bridge and came out the other side just in front,
then fought them all the way to the finish. It was
great. We had so much power, rating 32 and
storming home like seals on steroids. Warrington
first, University second, Girls Grammar third and
the water foamed around us like champagne.*

I'm also proud of the scene where Sophie and Lisa
combine forces to nail some younger kids who are
picking on Marina. Even kids who are cruel or insensitive can show positive qualities, given the right
circumstances. Sophie is by no means all bad and
there are hints in *So Much to Tell You* that her tough-
ness is not the whole story. There are other reasons
for her behaviour.

In fact one of the most important things for me in
Take My Word for It was to show that there can be many
perspectives within one story and they can all be
'true'. When we read *So Much to Tell You* we empathise
with Marina and sympathise with her because what
happened to her is so appalling, but we also feel for
her because she is the protagonist, and we tend to
sympathise with main characters regardless of their
attractiveness or integrity. In *Take My Word for It* I
wanted to show that the truth about Marina might be

a little more complex. For example, in *So Much to Tell You* she angrily denies stealing from the other girls. In *Take My Word for It* we are led to believe that she probably did steal.

So Much to Tell You

MARCH 2

Things aren't exactly good for me here, you know. And nothing seems to help. Including writing it all down. I got accused of stealing on Wednesday. But I didn't do it.

Take My Word for It

FEBRUARY 27

Wow, the fan sure got splattered tonight. Kate caught Marina with one hand in her locker and Kate's Rock City shirt in the other. Kate went off like a space shuttle, grabbed Marina and chucked her half way across the dorm, yelling and screaming as only Kate can. As soon as Marina got a chance she snuck out of the dorm and disappeared, which turned out to be a major problem when we couldn't find her again. Eventually we had to tell Mrs Graham, and the prefects got sent out to search. They found her in the Bag Room having a nervous breakdown, so now she's in Sick Bay for the night, and we're all in trouble.

It beats me how Marina can steal stuff and yet we end up in trouble.

Living with Marina would be difficult and would put a great strain on the other girls in the dormitory, and we don't get an adequate sense of that in *So Much to Tell You*. In *So Much to Tell You* Lisa seems cold and strong; in *Take My Word for It* we realise that there is more to her. Underneath she has great sensitivity and perception.

It's fantastic to get letters from girls who say that the book is accurate in its depiction of their lives. Writing fiction always requires a leap of the imagination and when I read these letters I can be hopeful I've made the leap successfully.

Chapter Three

The Great Gatenby

Authors and publishers talk about 'the second-book syndrome'. What they mean is that when someone has written one book, and it's been successful, the second book can become a burden. How do you write something that will live up to the first? How do you write something which is fresh and doesn't just repeat the plot or ideas of the first?

It's said that everybody has one book in them; the story of their own life. So in theory, writing one book shouldn't be too difficult. It's the second book, where you have to range more widely and make your imagination work more energetically, that's the real challenge.

Luckily I'd never heard of the second-book syndrome. If I had, it might have paralysed me, as it has done many writers over the years.

I was staying with some friends at The Rock, near Wagga Wagga in NSW. The Montagues were a friendly, cheerful family, with four daughters. I wanted to entertain them. I guess someone else might have played the piano, or done tricks, or told jokes. But the only way I know to entertain people is through stories and language. So I wrote them a story. It was the first chapter of *The Great Gatenby*. Luckily, they laughed when they read it, and the laughter didn't seem too fake or polite. So I kept going with the second chapter. If they hadn't laughed I wouldn't have gone any further.

The Great Gatenby was based partly on a group of boys who had been students at Timbertop when I was teaching there. Dave Downey, Sam McLeish and Stuart Powney were the kind of students who drive every teacher crazy. They were fun-loving, disobedient, casual. They refused to take anything seriously, or to conform to anything, including rules. They were also funny, irrepressible and entertaining. As a teacher, they drove me crazy. But I enjoyed their creative approach to school life, and even while sentencing them to detentions, I was hoping I wouldn't crush their spirit.

After the year ended, and we all survived, I moulded them into one character, and called him Erle Gatenby.

A popular theme in literature over the years has been the experiences and difficulties of an individual placed in a society where he is an outsider, a foreigner. That is the situation Erle finds himself in at the start of the book. The same premise is used in movies like *Crocodile Dundee*. The world of boarding schools can be a strange one, inhabited by strange characters, and full of bizarre rules and rituals. Although I lived in that world for many years, I never ceased to be fascinated by its odd practices, and I guess that too shows in *Gatenby*.

Of the characters in my books, Erle is one of the ones most like me. I wasn't good at swimming – in fact, I sank like a stone every time I went near water – and I wasn't as quick and smart and cool as Erle, but I did have his disrespect for authority and his capacity for getting in trouble. Maybe that's another reason I enjoyed teaching Stuart and Sam and Dave.

The Great Gatenby required the least imagination of any of my books. Not only did I have memories of my own school days, I also had my experiences as a teacher. I'd guess that ninety per cent of the book is true. Often nowadays when I'm speaking to high-school audiences and at the end of the speech there's time for questions, some smart alec asks: 'Is the scene on page 104 of *The Great Gatenby* from your imagination or from real life?'

Of course they are referring to Erle's sexual exploits with his luscious girlfriend Melanie, and I usually give an evasive answer. But nearly all the stuff Erle does, and the things that happen to him, come from real life.

For example, I remember a student named Simon Hutchings at Timbertop telling me about the gastro epidemic, which put half the school into the sanatorium. To entertain themselves as they started to recover, they held a farting competition, the rule being that whoever poohed his pants last was the winner. I've forgotten who won, but Simon later admitted he had cheated – and he had the evidence to prove it. This experience went into the book pretty much unchanged.

I also remember a student called Sam Austin, a big strong boy, who, while the others were collecting large logs for firewood, came back with a handful of twigs. I said to him: 'Sam, I've got toothpicks at home bigger than those logs.' He replied: 'Yes, but you've got such a big mouth.'

And so another paragraph was added to the book.

The scene where Melanie appears at boarding school wearing different-coloured nail polish on each of her fingers came from an episode I witnessed on my first day at Geelong Grammar. The girl was a feisty and spirited student named Anna Brown. The woman she clashed with was a teacher who reacted to Anna with much more strength than did the housemaster in the book.

James is based on a young man named Adam Furphy; the swimming coach is based on a terrific teacher named Tom Ashton, who is a thoroughly nice human being, but whom I painted in aggressive terms to add tension to the story; Ringworm is based on a boy whom I'd better not name, but who wandered into my flat in the boarding house in the middle of the night to complain, 'My brain's hurting'. The conversation as described in the book is pretty much a verbatim transcript.

The incident where Ringworm washes his hair with shampoo 'for dry hair only' happened when I was teaching at All Saints' College in Bathurst. The boy was a lovely innocent kid named Steven Silversmith, known as 'Silverhobbit', who died at a tragically young age.

Melanie is an invented character, but the sadness and emptiness of her life, and the way in which she is sent to boarding school by parents who don't care much about her, were all too true of a number of students I taught.

The description of her house is taken as accurately as I can remember it from the home of the Myer family in Toorak, Victoria. I visited the house only once, and reacted pretty much the way Erle does in the book, being overwhelmed by its grandeur. I sent a copy of the book to the Myers when it was published, thinking they might be amused to see their house written up in a novel, but they never wrote back. Perhaps they were offended. I'm not sure if a house can sue for defamation, but this one didn't. The Myers themselves were killed in a plane accident in Alaska a few years later; a great loss to Australia, as they were fine people, and generous members of the community.

It's been a running joke of mine since *The Great Gatenby* to mention Tozers' Department Stores in as many books as I can. A couple of observant readers have noticed it, but it's really only something I do to amuse myself, perhaps in the same way that film director Alfred Hitchcock managed to sneak his own image into every movie he made. There are Tozers' Department Stores in Wirrawee and Stratton, as well as in *Dear Miffy*.

The ending of the book came from another family of friends with whom I was staying, in Sydney this time. The Utz family at Mosman also had four daughters. One of them was enjoying a good relationship with her boyfriend. One afternoon she came home to a note stuck on her bedroom door by her mother. The note said: 'Simon rang; said he doesn't want to see you anymore. PTO.'

On the back Mrs Utz had added: 'On the other hand, if you still want to keep going out with him, he'll pick you up at seven o'clock tonight.'

I thought it was very funny, and it gave me the conclusion I wanted.

When the book was finished I took it to Walter McVitty Books, the publishers of *So Much to Tell You*. McVitty seemed to think the book was too lightweight for his name to be associated with it, although he also said I would have no trouble getting it published. I then took it to Penguin, who after some consideration decided not to publish it, and recommended I try Pan Macmillan. I sent it to them, and waited anxiously for an answer.

A few months later I got two letters on the one day. The first was from Pan Macmillan, and it began with a sentence I have always treasured: 'Everyone here at Pan Macmillan loves *The Great Gatenby*.' The warmth and generosity of these words made a great impression on me, and I hardly noticed that they were offering only five hundred dollars for the book. In the same mail was a letter from *Australian Wild*, a prestige glossy magazine dealing with the outdoors, offering to publish a poem I had sent them. I think they paid me a hundred dollars. Getting the two letters on the same day was a wonderful moment, and made me realise that I could probably make a go of professional writing.

The poem, incidentally, was later turned into the picture book *Norton's Hut*, published by Lothian Books in 1998, and illustrated by the Tasmanian artist Peter Gouldthorpe.

Later I heard the story of how Pan Macmillan

came to publish *The Great Gatenby*. They had appointed a new editor, Penny Hueston, and gave her a huge pile of manuscripts to look through. One was mine. It was almost the first one she read, and she rang Pan Macmillan straight away saying: 'This is great! We must publish this!'

They thought: 'Ah yes, in her enthusiasm for her new job, and with her limited experience, she is making a common mistake – thinking every submission she reads is worth publishing.'

So they told her to go away and have another look, and another think, and to read a lot more manuscripts. However, she was adamant that this one was worth it, and she finally persuaded other people in the company to have a look. Luckily they agreed with her when they read it.

The strangest postscript to *The Great Gatenby* came when a woman researching a real-life Gatenby family contacted me. She wrote saying that she had not heard of this particular branch of the family, and could I please supply her with more details. I had to write back and explain that they were fictional. Oddly enough, there was a student at Geelong Grammar with the surname Gatenby, who was there when I wrote the book; but the school is so vast, with four different campuses, that I had no knowledge of her.

One of the nicest souvenirs I have from writing came from *The Great Gatenby*. A woman in Sydney gave me a photo of her son reading the book by torchlight. She explained that her son had been a reluctant reader; that in fact he hated books. But one day she gave him a copy of *Gatenby*. A few hours later there was a power cut, and as she went through the house looking for candles, she found her son avidly reading the book by torchlight. She forgot about the candles and went for her camera instead, and I was delighted to get a copy of the resultant photograph. As every writer would agree, nothing beats the delight of converting someone who doesn't like books.

The Great Gatenby remains a happy book for me, and a personal favourite. Occasionally students even mistake it for its far more illustrious predecessor *The Great Gatsby*, which makes me smile, and perhaps justifies my cheek in giving the book such a presumptuous name.

Chapter Four

The Journey

Under the influence of Canadian English teacher John Mazur, in Bathurst in the late 1970s, I became interested in North American Indians. (In fact, I ended up knowing more about them than I did about Australian Aborigines, which is a sad reflection on my education.) However, I had always been interested in other cultures – I remember having a furious argument in 1969 with the grandmother of one of my friends, when she insisted that Australian Aborigines were primitive and ignorant.

The more I looked at other cultures, the more I felt that ours was inadequate. The destructive influence of the Anglo-Saxon race on other societies was apparent in every corner of the world. There is an arrogance about the English which is redeemed only by their sense of humour. When that arrogance is combined with the shallowness and crassness of American culture, the results are not pretty, and it seemed to me that this was how white Australian society was in danger of evolving.

Some of the things that have been vital in every human society, presumably since the beginning of the species, are the existence of a spiritual dimension, respect for death and the dead, appreciation of music and art, a need for courage and strength, the importance of storytelling, and the necessity for coming-of-age ceremonies.

As a teacher working with young people, I was particularly interested in the last of these. In other societies, initiation ceremonies often involved going through an ordeal, or responding to a great challenge, in order to prove one's worth as an adult. So, for example, these ceremonies included painful experiences like face carving, body carving, knocking out front teeth, or circumcision. In some North American Indian tribes, a young person would spend days alone in the desert and come back to report to the elders on what he had seen and experienced. These accounts had great significance for the tribe, and were interpreted by the elders, so their meaning could be understood by all.

When I looked at contemporary Australia I saw a very different picture. In my youth the most important initiation ceremony was that of confirmation in the Christian Church, which had been a significant experience for me, but which had lost meaning for most Australians as we became a more secular society. Other rites of passage also seemed to be losing their meaning, or disappearing altogether: the debutante ball; the twenty-first birthday party; even a boy's graduation into long pants, and a girl putting her hair up.

None of these events was as painful, or perhaps as powerful, as body scarring or circumcision, but they had definite meaning, and the meaning was understood by all.

The 'ceremonies' which seem to have replaced them are graduation from primary school, graduation from high school and perhaps from university, and the attainment of the eighteenth birthday, which brings with it the right to vote and to drink alcohol. But I consider it a disturbing aspect of our culture that most young people can become adults merely by staying alive and having birthdays. In most societies it was not enough to reach a particular age; one also had to pass tests. In our society the only tests are the Year 12 and tertiary exams and the one to get a driver's licence. These are the last vestiges of the initiation ceremonies of other cultures, but they are hardly enough to replace the extraordinary and powerful rituals that North American Indians and Australian Aborigines, amongst others, developed.

I was still teaching at Timbertop while I wrote *The Journey*. Working there had a powerful effect on me. I was staggered at the range and difficulty of the programme. The hikes were over some of the most difficult and dangerous country in Australia, through weather conditions that could range from forty-degree heat to snow blizzards, with students navigating for themselves, covering vast distances, and hardly seeing an adult the whole time. Virtually every student achieved these goals.

I do not want to idealise the programme, because there were faults with it, and at times it was too severe for many students; but they got through it, some brilliantly, some painfully. Afterwards most described it as the best year of their lives. What impressed me was their growth in self confidence and maturity. It reinforced a belief I already held: that the best achievements come through struggle and, sometimes, the greater the struggle, the more meaningful the achievement. It also taught me that we were underestimating young people; that they were capable of extraordinary feats. In many parts of Australia teenagers were not trusted to cross the road on their own, yet at Timbertop the same young people, from a range of backgrounds, a range of ethnic origins, a range of cultures, and with a range of abilities, became competent bushmen and women in less than a year. Timbertop was a genuine initiation experience for most of its students.

Given this background, it is not difficult to see how *The Journey* came into existence. It was the third book I wrote, but the second one to be published; Pan Macmillan decided, after *So Much to Tell You* won the CBC Book of the Year Award in 1988, that *The Journey*, being more serious than *The Great Gatenby*, should be my next published work.

As usual, the book had many influences. One was the work of the German writer Hermann Hesse, whose books, particularly *Siddhartha* and *The Glass Bead Game*, had been very powerful for me. Another, as I have already mentioned, was my understanding of other cultures. The huge numbers of fables and myths I read in childhood were a strong influence, as was *The Uses of the Imagination*, by Bruno Bettleheim. A wonderful old book by Dan Mannix called *Memoirs of a Sword Swallower* gave me background about the lives of 'freaks' in the old travelling fairs, and caused me to reflect on the nature of people who are 'different'.

I began writing *The Journey* on a bus trip to Melbourne, when I was supervising the Timbertop students on their return home at the end of a term. Argus is based on a student named James Laycock, whom I had enjoyed teaching, and who had a fresh and honest approach to life. He was starting to engage with the world in the same way as Argus in the book, and to explore some of the same issues.

Names were especially important in this book. Argus is of course based on the name of the ship that Jason commanded on his quest for the Golden Fleece. Ifeka is a corruption of Ithaca, the home of Ulysses. In ancient Greek legend Tiresias was a blind man with special insight who had also been a woman; in *The Journey* he represents the ambiguity of all people. The town of Random is so called because it could be any town, anywhere. For the same reason the book is set in no time and no place. I wanted people to concentrate on the themes of the book rather than distance themselves by saying, 'Oh, this is all right for Europeans or Americans or Aborigines', or 'This was all right back in those days', or 'Maybe this is the way it will be some time in the future'. I did the same thing in *Tomorrow, When the War Began*, which could be set in any Australian state.

The Journey begins with Argus leaving home, an event which his parents resist, as do most parents. But it is essential in the development of all young people that they leave home when the right time comes; in our society most young people seem to be staying at home for too long. The men Argus meets along the way are all father figures to him in their different forms, just as the men Jack meets in 'Jack and the Beanstalk' (including the Giant) can be seen as manifestations of his father.

Sexual experiences are part of everybody's life, but quite a number of people objected to my writing about them so explicitly in *The Journey*. When I look back at the book now, the sexual descriptions seem quite restrained. But one librarian commented to me at the time that they were too sensual, too erotic. Perhaps she thought young people should always have sex described to them in clinical or unloving terms. I chose to show sex as a positive, enjoyable experience, to counter the way it is often presented to young people as frightening and dangerous.

I was once accused by a Year 9 student at a private boys' school of writing pornography in *The Journey*, but when I talked to the teacher afterwards, it emerged that the boy was eleven years old, and was in Year 9 as part of an accelerated program for intellectually gifted children. I felt that perhaps he was not yet old enough to appreciate the sexual dimension of the story.

The death of Argus's sister perhaps reflects my own anxiety about the serious illnesses of my younger sister when I was a child, a topic I revisited in *Out of Time*.

The episode where the baby is taken is a reaction to a newspaper article I read about the disappearance of Azaria Chamberlain, at Uluru. Azaria was a baby taken from a tent by a dingo, and the whole of Australia became obsessed by the story and subsequent events. This was partly because of the accusations against the parents, who were suspected of having murdered the child, but also because of a primitive fear shared by us all, and described in the newspaper article as 'the fear of the snatching away of the baby'. I suppose the reason nature has endowed us with this primitive fear is so we will take more care to protect our babies, to be watchful parents. Understandably, it was a difficult and emotionally intense section of the book to write.

By the end of the book Argus's maturity is shown in a number of ways: not just because he has had sex, not just because he has grown older, but because he has taken on the responsibilities of a husband and father, and, ultimately, because he also takes on the responsibility of looking after his parents as they age. He has been tested and he has passed the tests.

The first story he tells at the end of the book is based upon 'Jack and the Beanstalk'. The giant reptile Slither represents the penis, as Bettleheim argues the beanstalk does in Jack's story. The story is really about the tendency of adolescent boys to become absorbed by sex and their penis, and the need to grow beyond this stage – as I discussed more explicitly in *Secret Men's Business*. The second story is not just about a foolish and irresponsible man, but also about the licence that can be taken with stories, thus reminding us of their unreliability. It's a warning to readers not to take any stories, including mine, too literally. The third story, brief as it is, suggests that we should not be constricted by notions of time or age. In particular it refers to the way we place too much value on chronological age. If there is one thing I've learnt in my life it is that wisdom and ignorance can be found among people of any age: I've met plenty of wise ten year olds and plenty of ignorant ones; and I've met plenty of wise old people, and plenty of stupid ones.

The thinking behind Alzire's story, the fourth story in the last section of the book, will be easily understood by anyone who has read the works of the great Swiss psychologist Carl Jung. Alzire's shadow is part of herself, the dark forces within her, which will take her over if she allows it. Alzire has to confront the dark side of her own soul and use her strength and goodness to combat it. She can never destroy or eradicate it, but she can make sure that it does not control her.

The fifth story also plays with the idea of conflicting forces within ourselves. Although we are unique in special and wonderful ways, we are also unique in our individual freakishness. The person who understands this and can come to terms with it is wise indeed.

The sixth story is about the journey from ignorance to wisdom, from a narrow-minded perspective to true understanding. It is in a real sense the journey from childhood to adulthood. The story starts with a baby, living on a primitive level. Through his experiences, and his willingness to listen and learn, he reaches maturity.

The last story, the poem, is self explanatory, although the last line: 'And a road that wants walking again', refers to my belief that we must keep revisiting our past if we are to understand ourselves.

The Journey was strongly supported by Pan Macmillan publisher James Fraser. He might well have backed away from such an unconventional and controversial book but instead he committed to it and helped it to find a readership.

One of the greatest pleasures from the publication of *The Journey* has been that other creative people have been influenced by it. A Sydney composer wrote music for an operatic version of the book, although unfortunately the opera was never produced. A Melbourne artist created a range of pictures inspired by the book. And I have been sent poems and stories by people who used the book as a springboard for their own writing.

The Journey was a long and difficult book to write, as there were so many stories to tell and so many ideas to explore. Yet I am proud of it, and for many people it is their favourite of my books. People tend either to love it or hate it: it polarises readers more than most of my other work.

Chapter Five

Out of Time

American writer Robert Cormier, in a speech at a Children's Book Council conference in Sydney, described his book *The Bumble Bee Flies Anyway* as his 'forgotten child'. He said it was his favourite of his own books, but not too many people seemed to share his opinion, and it hadn't sold many copies. After hearing his speech I went home and read *The Bumble Bee Flies Anyway*. I have to admit I didn't like it as much as his other books.

Out of Time is not my favourite of my own books, but I do have a soft spot for it, and not just because it is my least popular novel.

One of the reasons I wrote it was sheer bloody mindedness – not necessarily a good reason to write a book. The publisher Walter McVitty commented to me many times that a story must have 'a beginning, a middle and an end'. I've always objected to recipes, and I objected to this one. Postmodernism was a popular new movement among people interested in literature, and it made me rethink a lot of my attitudes. Postmodernist fiction mixes styles, moods, genres, and doesn't worry whether the story is original or whether it is 'high brow' or 'low brow'. Characters aren't warm or sympathetic or 'so real you feel you know them personally': they just are. Postmodernist books aren't sentimental or committed or passionate or 'deep'. They show the surface, and that's it. They seemed to me to demonstrate that a story does not need 'a beginning, a middle and an end'.

Out of Time is meant to work as a collage or mosaic. It is a patchwork of stories, all related. The main story comes to a conclusion, although many of the minor stories are left unresolved . . . to the possible frustration of the readers. But one of the great fascinations in life is the unresolved story. As long as I can remember I have been intrigued by the world's unsolved mysteries, like the Loch Ness Monster, the fate of the Tasmanian tiger, the story of the *Marie Celeste.*

When reading the *Book of Lists* one day, I chanced upon a paragraph which saddened me. It is used at the start of the novel, and it describes how the body of a child found in a circus fire in America has never been identified. Its identity remains a mystery to this day. Part of me longs for mysteries such as these to be solved, just as another part knows that the world would be a duller place if they were.

Among the mysteries that especially intrigue me are the missing-person stories. I think it's amazing the way a human being can vanish from the face of the earth. For example, in New Zealand, a country of three million, over 10,000 people are currently listed as missing.

Out of Time is about people who go missing; some of them physically, some of them emotionally. Many of the stories in the book come from real life; others from the imagination. The story of the American murderer in Melbourne, for example, is based loosely on an American serviceman in World War II, who came to Melbourne on leave and committed a series of killings known as the Brown-out Murders. The little boy in Mexico who may have survived a plane crash is based upon a story I read in a newspaper. And sadly, the disappearance of the Kalkadoon language, described near the end of the book, is all too true.

However, the story about the separated twins, the tale of the missing boy who can be seen in a photograph, and the account of the girl who loses her parents in the bomb blast are all made up.

The trip that James takes to an ancient civilisation in Central America is based on an article I read in *National Geographic* magazine; or, more precisely, its accompanying pictures. I tried to put into words the images suggested by an artist who illustrated the article.

The rewriting of the 'Dog on the Tuckerbox' legend, described by one reviewer as 'corny', is actually the true account of the incident. Of course it makes no sense to write a song about a dog that sits on a tuckerbox; but a dog that shits on a tuckerbox is much more likely to give rise to jokes or a song. So common sense alone suggests that this is what happened, and that the song has been sanitised by prudes who objected to the rude word, let alone the rude action. Similarly 'Waltzing Matilda' is believed to be about a swagman who does something much cruder to a sheep than steal it. Two policemen would not have bothered to ride so far to catch a swaggie who steals a sheep, nor would a swaggie commit suicide for such a trivial offence.

Although on the face of it *Out of Time* is science fiction, the time machine is just a literary device. The real theme I wanted to explore was the way in which we need to understand our past before we can understand our present – or have any influence on our futures. Using the time machine, James physically visits his past, in order to understand how the neglect by his parents, and his unjustified feelings of responsibility and guilt for the death of his sister, have affected him so strongly. The idea that one must make sense of the past to influence the future is also explored in *Take My Word for It* and *Letters from the Inside*, and is present to some extent in my other books.

Neglectful parents appear quite often in my books, including *Take My Word for It* and *Letters from the Inside*. Perhaps that's not surprising, after my teaching in boarding schools. Most of the stories of neglectful, insensitive or selfish parents in my writing are not made up.

The death of Ellie – a name I didn't realise I'd used already in *Out of Time* when I gave it to the main character in *Tomorrow, When the War Began* – is the specific event that James has to confront and understand. People who have been abused commonly feel that they contributed to the abuse. This trick that their minds play on them can be responsible for a lot of grief. James's guilt over his sister's death is not of course a rational response. Ellie dies because her parents were neglectful of her health and their responsibilities; although more subtle than beating or incest, neglect is abuse. Everything has been tangled into an ugly mess in James's head, and it seems no adult has made himself available to help straighten out his confusion, although there are suggestions that a few have tried. Mr Woodforde certainly tries, in a subtle and indirect way. He seems like a generous and wise man.

The idea of feeling guilty for things that aren't your fault is something I explored again in *Checkers*.

My younger sister, Rosalind, suffered from asthma as a child. She was hospitalised a number of times, and some of my earliest memories are of waiting outside hospitals, or visiting her when she was an in-patient. In particular, when we lived in Devonport, Tasmania, we went to Hobart for a holiday, and Rosalind had to be admitted to a Hobart hospital – extending our holiday, but not in a way which gave anyone any pleasure. I guess some of the anxiety, even fear for her life, that I felt back then resurfaced in this book. The episode in *Out of Time* which describes the family staying at a resort hotel when Ellie has to be hospitalised is an accurate description of that period, except my parents didn't spend their time in bars and casinos. The boy trying to ride the sheep does exactly what I did – in a paddock attached to the hotel where we were staying – at Kingston, I think. The story of the boy James cheers up in hospital is also true: when visiting Rosalind in the Hobart hospital, I spent a lot of time playing with a boy in the next bed, who was a couple of years younger than me and never seemed to receive any visitors. The Ward Sister remarked on how much he looked forward to my visits and how much I cheered him up. I was very proud of this at the time. I guess I was about nine years old.

In those days kids living in remote areas of rural Tasmania were often extremely isolated, and a boy admitted to hospital from one of those areas would not expect any visitors. Hobart wasn't much closer than the moon for backcountry families. Nan Chauncy wrote some wonderful books about Tasmanian families like these.

James in *Out of Time* shares with other characters in my books a refusal to speak. It seems difficult for me to write a novel without sneaking an elective mute in somewhere. The most obvious is Marina in *So Much to Tell You*, but less obvious are Wesley in *Staying Alive in Year Five*, and the feral children in the *Tomorrow* Series. Other relatively silent characters include Tony in *Dear Miffy*, the unnamed narrator in *Checkers*, and Tracey in *Letters from the Inside*.

As usual, in *Out of Time* I couldn't help putting in a few private jokes. The fictitious missing boy, Alexander Karatzann, in the story of the ghost in Castle Dundas goes missing on my birthday, 27 September. Nagged by my Year 7 English class of 1989 I finally relented and used their names in the book, even though none of them bore the slightest resemblance to the characters. I also plugged some of my favourite books, including Lee Harding's *Displaced Person*.

The main impetus in *Out of Time* is the suggestion that one must confront problems, and work at resolving them. The book ends on a positive and optimistic note, because James has taken charge of his life and addressed his worst fears. By revisiting the past, and willingly undergoing the pain involved, he is empowered to deal with his parents and himself, and thereby ensures a better future. Like Marina in *So Much to Tell You,* the time ahead of him will not be all roses and violins and chocolate. He'll have a lot of unhappiness and difficulty. But we can trust that both James and Marina, having made such progress, will probably find some satisfaction and pleasure in their adult lives.

Chapter Six

Letters from the Inside

In one of my old notebooks is a newspaper clipping about a girl who was sixteen when she found out her father had murdered her mother. The crime took place eight years earlier, but the girl was protected from the truth. She was told that her mother had died and her father had 'gone away'. She found out the true story accidentally, from reading an old newspaper.

This story stuck in my mind for a long time. Most of my books result from a number of stories which accumulate in my head, until gradually they start synthesising into the form of a novel. Eventually my head feels like it'll explode unless I start writing.

Another story that contributed strongly to *Letters from the Inside* was a conversation with a Year 12 student in a school where I was teaching. With the Christmas holidays about to begin I said to her: 'I guess you must be looking forward to a relaxing few months at home.'

She said: 'No, not at all.'

At first I thought she was joking, then I realised she was very serious. 'Why wouldn't you be glad to have a few months slacking around doing nothing?' I asked.

'Because of my brother.'

'Why, what's wrong with your brother?' I asked. I was still completely puzzled.

'He's so violent,' she said. 'I'm terrified of him. Whenever we're home alone he beats me up. Most days I lock myself into my room so that he can't get me.'

I stood there in horror. What made it even worse, in a way, was that her brother was several years younger than she was. (In the book I made him older, because I didn't think people would believe a younger brother could be so terrifying.)

When I made some enquiries later, I found she had cause to be concerned. Her brother had been suspended from school already for violence, and was known as a difficult and aggressive boy. I said to the girl: 'Have you told your parents about this? Why don't they do something?'

'I have told them,' she replied. 'But they say I'm exaggerating. Or they say it's just a typical stage boys go through. Or they say to ignore it, and he'll give up. But I know he won't. I've tried that and it doesn't work. If anything, it makes him worse.'

I could not stop thinking about this dark and troubling situation, and I was very concerned for the girl's safety. I was relieved to hear some time later that she was doing well and was living in a flat with friends, so the situation didn't end as disastrously as the one in *Letters from the Inside*.

Another incident that affected the book strongly

was a correspondence I enjoyed with a girl who had been expelled from the boarding school where I worked. An extremely intelligent girl, she had nonetheless been difficult, partly because of her chronic dishonesty. But I admired her for many other strengths; I enjoyed her sense of humour, and respected her intellect and rebellious spirit.

Some time after she had been expelled she wrote asking if she could come and stay with me for a weekend in my flat on the school campus. She explained that she wanted to visit her old friends in the boarding house. I wrote back and said that this presented too many problems. If for example she brought cigarettes or alcohol onto the campus and shared them with her friends, I would be put in a very difficult situation.

What surprised me was her response. She wrote back in a rage, asking: 'DON'T YOU TRUST ME?'

I thought: 'Well, no, of course I don't. Why should I?' She had lied to me in the past and, as I said, had a reputation for dishonesty. That didn't stop me liking her and enjoying the correspondence. But I still wasn't going to risk offering accommodation to her for a weekend.

It made me think about the way we present ourselves to others, and the way we believe others see us. It seems extraordinary that we can be so confident about our masks. Aggressive people believe they hide their aggression successfully; egoists believe they hide their vanity; liars believe they are able to fool people all the time, or that people have no memories.

Masks, and the realities behind them, are a source of constant fascination to writers. I would argue that every novel is to some extent about the gap between appearances and reality. I grew up in an Australia where masks were valued, and where good manners were considered more important than truth, so perhaps that made me all the more aware of masks, and all the more interested in them.

Another influence on *Letters from the Inside* was a book I read when I was young. It was called *Daddy-Long-Legs*, by Jean Webster, and it consisted of a series of letters written from a girl in an orphanage to an anonymous benefactor. The anonymous donor paid for her education, on condition that she wrote him a letter once a month, even though she was never allowed to know his identity. She wrote letters that were lively, spirited and feisty, but she was frustrated by the fact that she didn't know to whom she was writing, and hardly ever received an answer.

As the book unfolds, we realise she is writing to a man who appears quite often at the orphanage, but she doesn't realise he's her benefactor until the end of the book. They eventually fall in love and get married. There was a sequel called *Dear Enemy*.

Daddy-Long-Legs was turned into a musical starring Fred Astaire, but it was a long way removed from the book. I didn't like it much.

A few years ago I reread *Daddy-Long-Legs*. I was really disappointed. Some books hold up well, even after decades or centuries, but this one didn't. I was horrified by how controlling and manipulative, how jealous and possessive the man in the book is. I hadn't noticed that when I read it in the 1950s.

However, I was fascinated by the idea of letters being exchanged between people, where one writer has no real knowledge of the other.

Letters from the Inside came even closer to being written after I spent a week in Risdon Prison in Hobart. A major conservation campaign was underway to save the Franklin River, on Tasmania's west coast, from being dammed. The Hydro-electric Commission of Tasmania was a hugely powerful corporation that seemed to run the state. It appeared more powerful than the Government. Although Tasmania didn't need any more hydro-electric power, the commission seemed hell bent on building dams everywhere. Damming the Franklin would have caused terrible ecological consequences to one of the wildest and most beautiful parts of the world. The campaign to save the river became the most bitterly fought and important conservation battle in the history of Australia. I got involved in the early stages and eventually went down to the river to help protest against the actions of the Hydro-electric Commission.

I'd been there less than twenty-four hours when I was arrested and charged with obstructing a police officer and trespassing. At a preliminary hearing in Queenstown Magistrate's Court I refused to give an undertaking that I would not return to the Franklin, and so I was sentenced to a week in Hobart while I thought about it some more.

When we arrived at Risdon Prison it was announced that the Remand Section was full, and so I would be put in Maximum Security. I imagine that Chopper Read was probably in there at the same time, although I don't remember meeting him. I do remember the fear of being marched into Maximum Security, not knowing what was in store for me.

However, I survived the week, and it turned out to be valuable material for the prison scenes in *Letters from the Inside.* For instance, the incident where Jenelle might be charged with attempting to escape because she doesn't answer the roll correctly is a true story from my week in Risdon, and typical of the idiocies of institutional life.

> *The hacks are so raggy. Roll call this morning was a good one – Mrs Neumann was doing it. When she got to Jenelle Hawthorne, Jenelle just answered 'Yeah', instead of 'Present'. Mrs Neumann snapped. 'Right, you're charged: attempting to escape.' 'What?' said Jenelle. 'Yes,' said Mrs Neumann, frothing at the mouth. 'You didn't answer your name correctly, therefore you're not here. And if you're not here, you must be in Med Unit or attempting to escape.'*

Information about young people's maximum-security institutions came from a man who ran dog kennels in his spare time. I had booked my dog in there, without knowing anything about the owner, but when I arrived I was struck by the number of keys the man carried, and the number of locked doors and gates we had to go through before my dog reached his kennel. On the way out I asked the owner what he did, apart from running dog kennels. I shouldn't have been surprised by his answer: he worked in a maximum-security institution for teenagers.

By then I had started writing *Letters from the Inside* so I was delighted by this unexpected lead, and pumped him for information. However, I did think he was a little too fond of locking up living creatures, so I never took the dog there again.

As with every novel, I couldn't write *Letters from the Inside* until I had the right voice for the main character. In this book I needed three voices: the voice of Mandy, who had to sound like the girl next door, a typical Australian teenager; the false voice of Tracey, which had to sound too good to be true; and the real voice of Tracey.

I was doing some gardening near the back corner of my old house at Sandon in Victoria when suddenly I could hear the different voices. I threw down the shovel and hurried inside to get them on paper before they disappeared again. This experience is a familiar one to me, and an essential part of the writing process – perhaps the most essential part.

It was quite fun writing the letters in Tracey's false voice. It was nice to be able to indulge myself and write in a slightly mushy style, that was more reminiscent of Mills & Boon or *Sweet Valley High* than my usual writing. My only concern was that readers would start thinking the whole book was going to be a load of sentimental rubbish, and that they wouldn't persist with it.

How's it going with Paul? He sounds nice – I think you should go for it! I've been with my boyfriend for three months – his name's Casey Winter – he's gorgeous looking and really kind and loving but I don't know how much longer to keep it going. Three months is a long time! I don't want to get too serious, although he does.

I don't know what to suggest about earning money. My parents give me heaps of pocket money, plus they pay for my clothes and everything – my

*father says he wants me to look nice. So I don't
need much money.*

It was fun writing the revelation of Tracey's true identity, and I found myself getting increasingly drawn
into the mystery and suspense, and increasingly
caught up in the lives of the two girls. Tracey's world
seemed very real to me, perhaps as a result of my
week in Risdon, but perhaps also because much of my
life has been spent in institutions, especially boarding
schools.

It seems to me that the same kinds of concerns
prevail in all institutions: an obsession with food, an
obsession with the activities of the other people in the
institution, and a resentment of petty rules and regulations. So what I didn't know about prisons was easy
to make up.

The list of regulations on the wall of Tracey's cell
came straight from Risdon. I took their list with me as
a souvenir when I left, although I was worried that I
might be arrested again for stealing it. I put it into the
book unchanged, except for the deletion of 'one
razor blade' (because I didn't think people would
believe inmates of prisons were allowed razor blades)
and the addition of 'one packet tampons or sanitary
napkins'.

In telling Tracey's story, I wanted to show that under
the aggression and bravado was someone who had been
badly hurt. It is my belief there is no such thing as
crime, just illness. Happy well-balanced people don't
steal or assault or murder. It follows that anyone who
commits such acts must be unhappy and unbalanced. I
don't think we will be truly civilised as a society until we

recognise this and turn prisons into centres where people with these problems receive help and support to work through them. I didn't want readers to have sympathy for Tracey or other criminals; I wanted them to have understanding. Tracey is not a nice person, nor an attractive one. She is violent, full of rage and hatred, unwilling to face the truth or accept the consequences of her actions. As Mandy says, she wouldn't necessarily like to have Tracey move in with them.

I don't like to sentimentalise anything, including crime and criminals. But to understand them: that's a different matter entirely.

I also wanted people to realise that young men who are obsessively interested in guns and who talk a lot about violence are to be taken seriously. A teacher told me how she was driving along one day listening to her car radio, when a newsflash announced a gunman was shooting people at random in Hoddle Street, Melbourne. Her first reaction was: 'I bet it's Julian Knight' (or one other young man she had taught). She had always thought they were capable of this kind of violence. Yet she had done nothing about it.

I think that would be the same for most of us. From time to time we all meet people – generally men – who seem too violent, too aggressive. But we don't do anything about them, mainly because we don't know what to do, or we fear we might be overreacting. I didn't do anything about the violent younger brother of the girl who told me she was scared of him.

And so these attacks continue, often without causing any surprise to the people who know the attackers.

The paragraphs describing Mandy's brother Steve, in her final letters, are taken more or less directly from an inquest into Frank Vitkovic, a man who randomly shot eight Telstra employees in Queen Street, Melbourne, and then killed himself by jumping out of a window. At the inquest his sister was one of the main witnesses. She described her brother's behaviour in the last few days before his insane outbreak in much the same terms as Mandy describes Steve.

Another thing I wanted to do in *Letters from the Inside* was to celebrate the friendships enjoyed by girls. Television often presents these friendships as full of jealousy or bitchiness, or as something to be made fun of, but as a male and as a teacher I've always been impressed by the strong friendships girls have. They are often so supportive, so loving and generous. Such friendships are rare between males, and I suspect that many men envy them. Mandy's friendship with Tracey is important for both girls. Mandy learns a lot more about life and the universe; Tracey is softened, and begins to open up and relax, lowering her mask considerably as a result of Mandy's influence.

The ending of the book frustrates a lot of readers. Many get angry. I've had letters from readers describing how they threw the book against the wall when they finished, or saying that they took it back to the bookshop to see if they had a defective copy, or complaining that I had cheated – that I obviously couldn't think of an ending and so just left my readers up in the air. A couple of the letters were really abusive. Perhaps I should have been pleased the book made such an impact.

Letters from the Inside does have an ending. As with many of my books, I didn't know what that ending would be until I was halfway through. When I did realise, I put down my pen and sat there for a long time thinking, 'I can't write this. It's too terrible. The readers will kill me.' Then I thought, 'Well, I'll write it anyway, and maybe change it afterwards. I'll just keep going and see how it works out.'

So, I wrote it. And of course, once it was finished I couldn't change a word.

It always amazes me how the unconscious mind can be so far ahead of the conscious. My conscious mind didn't know in which direction the story was going; but my unconscious mind did, and when I read the first section back, I found quite a few clues to indicate that the story was always heading that way. It had just taken me a long time to see it.

So, what went through my mind that day was: 'Mandy dies, and Tracey never finds out.'

There are many details which make it clear that this is the ending. In my scenario, Steve kills the whole family at three a.m. on Boxing Day. Tracey wakes up at that time, screaming, after a horrifying and violent dream. She and Mandy are so bonded that when something bad happens to Mandy, Tracey feels it. The whole family has to be dead, because otherwise it's unbelievable that no one would respond to Tracey's letters. They knew about Mandy's friendship with her, and they would not have been so cruel as to leave Tracey on her own, in ignorance. No-one answers the letters because there's no-one left alive to answer them.

I deliberately transferred the only kind warder, Miss Gruber, out of the institution just before Christmas, so that the one person Tracey could ask for information wasn't there for her.

The reference to the *Diary of Anne Frank* is another clue. Anne was a real-life teenager who died in tragic circumstances; another victim of violence.

Tracey of course does know unconsciously, and almost consciously, what has happened. In her last letters she keeps saying: 'I know you're not all right.' Tracey has been around violence all her life; she's familiar with it, she's seen how it works, she understands its consequences.

Among the suggestions I've had from readers about Mandy's fate are: Tracey is schizophrenic and is writing all the letters in the book and Mandy is just a manifestation of her illness; Tracey has a psychiatrist or counsellor who is writing the letters, pretending to be Mandy; Mandy moved away (but that's no reason for her to stop writing); Mandy's parents forbade her to write anymore (but at least she would have written to Tracey and told her that was the case); Mandy's sister, working in the post office, intercepts the letters, so Mandy never gets them (I suppose it's possible but it's a bit far fetched).

I have to admire the ingenuity and imagination of readers in coming up with so many explanations, but I think deep down many of them know Mandy's fate. When I ask them: 'What do you think happened?' they often look worried and say, 'Did something bad happen to Mandy?' So they are very close to the truth, but because they like her they don't want to believe that Steve could have killed her. I certainly sympathise with them.

The real reason Mandy dies – in an abstract sense – is that Tracey has never expressed contrition for her crime. The reader doesn't know what Tracey's done, and neither do I, but we know it's very serious. She's probably killed someone, or hurt someone badly. As I was writing the book I kept thinking, 'I must at some stage reveal Tracey's crime,' but I could never bring myself to do it. I think I liked her so much I didn't want to know what she'd done.

Since the book was published I've had a number of invitations to run workshops in prisons. When I go there I always make sure I have no information about the prisoners before, during or after the workshops, as I don't want to feel negative in my dealings with them. I don't want to be put off. It was the same in writing about Tracey: I didn't want to be put off by the knowledge of whatever horrifying act she had committed.

So the book has a moral balance: people like Mandy, innocent people, keep dying because people like Tracey can't accept the consequences of their actions, can't confront the reality of their lives. As long as the Traceys of the world don't take any responsibility, the Mandys of the world will keep getting killed.

Many people called the book immoral, because it contains swear words, and the occasional crude remark, but their definition of morality seems narrow to me. *Letters from the Inside* is a very moral book indeed.

When I finished it I rang the publishers and said: 'I never want to write another book like this. It's too disturbing.' When I was editing it, I still felt it was disturbing, but I liked the way it flowed, and rather conceitedly perhaps said to the same publisher, 'I can never write better than this.'

The reactions to it were certainly strong. Generally, adults feared and loathed the book, although that's not to say a lot of them didn't enjoy it; and as the years have gone on, perhaps adults have become more appreciative of it. Teenagers responded powerfully and positively, and I was struck, as I have been many times since, by the fact that young readers react so differently to older readers, but older readers don't seem to notice that.

'Although I can't completely relate to them both, I understood the way they felt and thought, once something had gone wrong or something bad happened.' (Marnie, 13)

'When I read this book I almost started crying, as it was so heart-breaking and I know that it has to be one of the best books ever written.' (Vicky, 12)

'I felt sorry for Tracey, how her days were spent in misery. I cried in some parts and laughed in others. I was reading this on the holidays about 11 p.m. and it really freaked me out, when I found out about Tracey in the detention centre.' (Megan)

'Thank you for writing a book that has never forced upon me such strong, loving emotions.' (Allison, USA)

'It makes me wonder what I would do in that situation; whether I would be a friend to someone who confused me by giving me all different information, and I wonder if I would trust someone who did that to me.' (Sophie)

Chapter Seven

Tomorrow, When the War Began

'The pace of the story at times is tediously slow . . . it falls far short of the claims made for it by its publishers, that it is the most powerful book ever published in this country for teenagers.'

'I read the first few chapters, but to be honest I found it too slow and didn't bother going on with it.'

These were the first two adult reviews of *Tomorrow, When the War Began*.

The first came from a magazine specialising in reviews of children's and adolescent fiction. The second came from an ABC radio broadcaster, to whom I had sent an advance copy of the book.

Yet to weigh against these reactions was the response of my editor, Julia Stiles. Editors are trained from birth to react positively to novelists. They know how to be supportive and encouraging. But I've never heard a response like Julia's, when she read *Tomorrow, When the War Began*. I came home after doing the shopping, saw the red light flashing on the answering machine, pressed the button and out came Julia's voice, at a volume that filled the room.

'It's amazing,' she yelled. 'It's wonderful . . . fantastic . . . unbelievable! You've written a classic. This book will change teenage fiction for ever.' When it was published she wrote to me saying, 'Well, here it is at last, a book destined to become an Australian classic.'

And, perhaps more important than Julia's reactions, was my own gut feeling as I was writing.

Tomorrow, When the War Began began when I was a little kid. Like most kids, probably all kids, I resented the control adults had over my life. I got sick of being told what to do and when to do it, what not to do, and how I should be. I daydreamed occasionally of a world where the adults miraculously disappeared. In my daydreams I didn't bother to explain where they'd gone; I just imagined a situation where kids were in charge of everything. I never thought about it lasting more than a few days, and most of my fantasies were to do with getting into milk bars and helping myself to Rainbow Monsters and Choo-choo bars. I seem to remember the idea of being able to help myself to a car was pretty attractive too.

Years later I found a novel called *The Girl Who Owned the City*, which, according to the blurb, was about a city without adults, run entirely by kids. Even as an adult I felt the power of such a scenario and I bought the book. It was awfully disappointing, as it turned out to be propaganda for some obscure political movement. But it does illustrate how that childhood dream was still somewhere in the back of my mind as an interesting and powerful scenario.

Another influence in writing the book was my awareness of what happened in World War II. I was born years after the war ended, but I was brought up with the knowledge that my father fought in North Africa, Borneo and New Guinea, as an officer in the Australian Army. He was shot in the upper leg, but recovered and went on to fight some more. I still have the pack he was wearing that day, with the bullet hole through it.

I also knew that the Japanese Armed Forces had come much closer to Australia than was comfortable. I knew that Darwin had been heavily bombed, that Broome and Thursday Island had been bombed, and that even Townsville had suffered an attack, resulting in one cracked window, and a coconut being shaken from a palm tree.

In 1942 Japanese midget submarines snuck into Sydney, evading the anti-submarine net hung between the two heads of the harbour. The subs attacked some Australian vessels, sinking the 'Kuttabul' and causing many deaths. Meanwhile, off the coast, the mother submarine was shelling houses in the expensive and exclusive eastern suburbs of Sydney.

Those Japanese midget submariners were brave men. They knew they would die on this mission, and they did. It's to the credit of the Australian Government and the Australian people that the Japanese men were honoured as heroes and given a full ceremonial burial in Sydney. Even their victims recognised their courage.

I thought a lot about the war one Anzac Day as I watched a parade in Melbourne. Many of the marchers were very old, struggling along on walking frames or walking sticks. As I looked at them, and at the cheering crowds, I wondered about the meaning of the event. We were hailing these people as heroes. Yet what had they done? Surely most of them just reacted to the events that happened around them. If your country is at war, your options become limited. You can't go for overseas holidays, you can't pig out on exotic imported food, you can't buy a new Rolls Royce. Everybody has to make sacrifices. Everybody is restricted. Everybody has to put aside private needs and greeds for the public interest. The Government, backed by the police and the armed forces, generally ensures that this happens. So if you're tempted to be selfish or greedy, it's made difficult for you.

All kinds of pressures are put on people to join the fighting. In many countries, including Australia at different times in her history, men are forced to join the armed forces. Those who refuse can be punished severely.

On the other hand some people are exceptional. Some do far more than they have to. They volunteer for tough assignments, act with extraordinary heroism, suffer great adversity.

But these people are a minority. I could safely say, looking at the Anzac Day parade, that the majority of people in it would not fall into that category. Most of them simply *did what had to be done.*

Of course some lost the plot badly. For example, when the Japanese Air Force bombed Darwin heavily – and effectively – many members of the Australian Armed Services ran like rabbits. One man got as far as Melbourne, doing the trip in only thirteen days. Many of those who stayed spent their time vandalising and looting.

I looked at the young people in the Anzac Day crowd. Many teenagers were there. It was great to see them showing respect and appreciation for the sacrifices of their grandparents. But I wondered, looking at them, what would happen if the dates for the war had been different.

If the Second World War had started three years ago, and ended last week, presumably the roles would be reversed. The old people would be in the crowd, grateful and moved, cheering the heroism and sacrifices of the young people. The young people would be marching down the street, heads high, medals on their chests.

And yet many people were willing to say that today's teenagers would not conduct themselves with spirit or courage, but would run home and hide under their beds if faced by physical challenges or great danger. So the main thing I wondered, looking at the crowd, was how today's teenagers would react in the event of a war. Would they dig deep and find reserves of initiative, maturity, responsibility and even heroism that they were perhaps not aware of themselves?

Thinking about the answer was one of the major forces that drove me to write *Tomorrow, When the War Began*. I thought the book might be a chance to counter the bad press teenagers get. According to the popular media, every teenager in Australia is either illiterate, drug crazed, suicidal, alcoholic, criminal, promiscuous, selfish, a dole bludger, or all of the above.

Another issue for me was the security of Australia. I have no political barrow to push, and I know next to nothing about our defence and security arrangements, but it amazes me that we never talk about these issues. We fondly imagine that we live in a perfectly safe country, but history suggests we shouldn't be so complacent. It is a rare country that has gone fifty years without being invaded. The fact that Australia has had such a long run without a direct military threat is as much luck as good management, but it's not something we can rely on for ever.

A teacher in Wagga, asking a question from the audience after I'd finished speaking about *Tomorrow, When the War Began*, said: 'One of my students was very upset and frightened after reading the book, and she asked me if I thought Australia might ever be invaded.'

I said: 'I hope you didn't reassure her.'

'Well, yes, I did actually,' he replied, looking a bit embarrassed.

'I don't think you did her any favours,' I said. 'I don't want to traumatise anyone, or make anyone paranoid, but I think we should be realistic and give some thought and attention to defence. It's likely that during the lifetime of today's teenagers they will have to face some kind of pressure or threat from somewhere, so we should be talking about it and making preparations for it.'

In recent times, only the aftermath of the independence referendum in East Timor has made Australians think about these issues.

As with my other novels, the main spark came with the voice of the narrator. I found Ellie's voice quite unexpectedly, as I drove back from the tip one Saturday afternoon. I was in an old Land Rover, just five hundred metres from home, and suddenly I could hear Ellie talking.

*It's only half an hour since someone, Robyn I
think, suggested we write this down. And it's only
five minutes since I got chosen. But I can't do it
while they're all crowded around me, yelling ideas
and advice. Rack off guys! Leave me alone!*

   *That's better. Now I'm down at the creek. I
don't know why they chose me to do this. I guess
I'm meant to be good at English or something . . .*

Realising that if I didn't get her voice on paper, I
might lose it again for ever, I pulled off to the side of
the road, grabbed an old envelope that was blowing
around in the back of the Land Rover, and quickly
wrote down the words.

I drove on to my place, parked the Landy, and
raced into the house knowing that I had a new book
underway, and feeling very excited about it. Those
original words were altered quite a bit as I edited the
book, but the tone and style never changed.

As with all my characters, Ellie formed herself
around her voice. But she was based quite strongly on a
student I'd taught on a number of occasions. Charlotte
Austin was a boarder at Geelong Grammar School when
I started working there in the early 80s. She was in Grade
6, and was in a small group of advanced Grade 6 kids I
took for writing workshops, once a week. Although I was
a full-time secondary teacher it was refreshing and exciting to work with such bright students. Later, when I was
teaching Year 9 at Timbertop, I had Charlotte in one of
my English classes for the whole year. And then later
again, when I was teaching at the main campus back in
Geelong, Charlotte was one of the stars of a fascinating
and brilliant Year 12 English class.

It was most unusual to have taught someone at so many stages of her life, but as a child, as a teenager and as an adult, Charlotte was memorable. She came from a large property in the Riverina, and had a strength of character that deeply impressed me. She was resourceful, imaginative, mature, and honest. She was also an outstanding writer, with a lively style, a keen intelligence, and a willingness to take risks.

In the Trial VCE English exam, halfway through Year 12, Charlotte had to write four essays, which were marked by four different English teachers from the Geelong Grammar staff. Her total mark was 48 per cent.

I read the essays, which I thought were fantastic, then I said to Charlotte: 'I think they're wrong. But I may be the one who's wrong. You can either conform to the standard traditional style of essay, and guarantee yourself an A, or you can keep writing the way you always have, with your own distinctive approach, in which case I think you'll get a huge mark. But it is a bigger risk.'

Charlotte didn't hesitate. 'I'm happy with the way I write,' she said, 'and I'm not changing for them.'

At the end of the year, in the VCE exam, marked outside the school by anonymous and independent examiners, Charlotte got 98 per cent.

I love telling this story, partly because I feel so smug about my role in it, but also because it is a good example of Charlotte's gutsy approach to life.

Not only was Charlotte mentally strong, she was physically strong too. After leaving school she did a building course and married Rick Lindsay, who makes rammed-earth buildings. She now runs a successful company with him, as well as operating her own design business.

Unlike Ellie, Charlotte was not stubborn or dominating, but I thought it would make Ellie a more complex and interesting character to give her those extra dimensions.

Ellie is also based on Norah Linton, a character in the famous Billabong books which I had enjoyed as a child. Norah lived on a big farming property, was courageous and resourceful, and got involved in many adventures. The books were unrealistic and simplistic, and wouldn't be enjoyed by so many young people today. And Norah was not allowed to be as adventurous as the boys, because of the attitudes towards females in those times. But within the limits of society in the early part of the twentieth century, Norah was a gutsy girl.

I loved the descriptions of farm life in the Billabong series. In recent decades most fiction for young people has been about city life, or suburban life, and the issues arising for families and kids in those situations. I've written some of those books myself, and I know and appreciate the need for them, but I thought it was a pity that we had gotten so far away from the bush and country novels that were popular in earlier generations, and I quite consciously set out to revive that genre.

Homer is based a little on another student I taught, a guy called James Bufton. James was very big for his age, physically strong, popular with girls, and from a rural background. I suppose one reason he stays in my memory is that he was involved in the only major broken bone of my life. We were crowbarring a log on the side of a hill when the log unexpectedly gave way, and I fell backwards, twisting as I did. I heard a horrible crack, felt a surge of pain, and knew I had broken my ankle. I rolled around on the ground, uttering obscenities the like of which many of the students had never heard before, while James and Charlotte Austin and others rolled around on the ground equally actively, except they were laughing. It took them a minute or so to realise I'd genuinely hurt myself. I suppose it's characteristic of my attitude towards Charlotte that I asked her to go and get a Land Rover and bring it up to me and drive me back to the school. She was fourteen years old at the time, but it never crossed my mind to doubt her competence. As it turned out though, another teacher was only a short distance away, and he drove me.

Incidentally, three years later, when I was watching a cricket match at Geelong Grammar, Charlotte, who was then in Year 12, rushed up to me and said: 'Quick, give me the keys to your Land Rover, don't ask any questions.' Thinking, 'This will be the end of my teaching career if anything goes wrong', I handed over the keys. I knew she wouldn't have asked for them unless she had a good reason. A few hours later she returned the keys. I never asked what she had needed them for, or where she had taken the car, and to this day I still have no idea.

Anyway, to get back to Homer. Again, Homer is very different to James Bufton. Most of my characters would be only ten or twenty per cent based on real people, although the correlation between Ellie and Charlotte is a bit higher. With Homer I especially wanted to create a character who was typical of many boys and girls from rural backgrounds whom I'd taught. At home they drove vehicles, ploughed fields, helped with shearing and harvesting and calving and lambing – and then went to boarding schools, where they were not trusted to change a light globe or put a Band-Aid on a cut. The contrast between these two dimensions of their lives was extraordinary, and it is to their credit that most of them handled it as well as they did, although for a number it resulted in frustration and anger. Homer's transition from annoying trouble-maker at school, to responsible leader away from school, is all too typical of these farm kids.

Corrie was based on Corrie Menzies, a girl I'd taught in Bathurst, although the resemblance between them is only a physical one.

Lee is based on a guy who became a good friend at university; a Chinese-Australian student named Phillip Ming-lai. I haven't heard of him for years, but I enjoyed his company very much, and admired his many gifts. But again the resemblance between the imaginary Lee and the real life Phillip is not strong.

Fi is based on two students whom I taught, Fiona Koch and Ellie Meleisa, whilst Robyn is a fictional re-creation of my older sister Robin. It had often seemed to me, looking at my sister's life, that she gave up a lot for others. She is perhaps the most self-sacrificing person I've met, to the extent that at times I worried about her own sense of self. I can see how Robyn's sacrifice in *The Third Day, the Frost* was an unconscious depiction of my concerns about my real-life sister. My sister is also a strongly committed Christian, but in recent years I think has become far more her own person, without losing her generosity or religious spirit.

I had decided some time earlier to try to include

a Christian character in one of my novels. A large number of young Australians are Christians, but you'd never know it from reading novels written for teenagers. They're a disenfranchised group. There are some Christian novels – usually awful – written to convert people, but I don't know of any mainstream Australian teenage novel with a Christian character.

Writing *Tomorrow, When the War Began* was an extraordinary experience. I'd read so many books about the war when I was growing up that the details about battles and tensions and emotions weren't difficult. For technical information about explosives, I called on my niece, Elizabeth Farran. At the age of twenty-four, Elizabeth had a shot firer's ticket, which meant she was legally qualified to blow up anything. Later, when I was writing *The Third Day, the Frost*, Elizabeth took me down into one of the Kalgoorlie mines and showed me supplies of the explosive anfo, so that I could handle it and smell it and get a good sense of what it was like.

The more I wrote the book, the faster I got. Wirrawee was a synthesis of country towns in which I'd lived, mainly Mansfield, Castlemaine and Newstead, but it also reminded me of many other country towns I'd visited. Some things in country towns are always the same, no matter which state you are in.

The novel kept getting bigger, which suited me fine. I wanted to write a big book, if only because I was sick of another insulting assumption about young people – that they wouldn't read anything longer than fifty pages. All the experts I spoke to said it was essential to give teenagers short books, because they wouldn't have the time or patience for anything longer. Yet everywhere I looked I saw teenagers avidly reading *Lord of the Rings*.

I got so engrossed in *Tomorrow, When the War Began* that I wrote the last twenty thousand words in three days. A neighbour, Al Watson, called in for coffee and a chat when I was halfway through the second-last chapter. I wanted desperately to keep writing but didn't like to turn away Al, who was a good friend. But after a few minutes of strained conversation I could stand it no longer and I said, 'Al, I'm sorry to be rude, but I'm totally engrossed in writing this book and I don't want to leave it even for a moment.' Al leapt to his feet, said, 'That's fine, I understand completely,' and dashed out the door. So I was able to resume work on the book and finish it without further disturbance.

As I was writing *Tomorrow, When the War Began* I became aware that this book had something special, and I became more and more certain that it would have a dramatic effect on readers. One of the reasons I wanted to finish it quickly was that I was terrified someone else would come up with the same idea and beat me to it. When I read the manuscript back, having at last completed it, I was excited by it more than anything else I'd ever written. I couldn't wait to get it to Pan Macmillan for their comments. It was I who suggested the caption 'The most powerful book ever written in Australia for teenagers' on the cover. That's a measure of how confident I was. But that comment, or 'shoutline' as it is called in the publishing industry, enraged a lot of experts in young people's literature. They wanted to be the ones to say which novels were powerful and which were not. They didn't like being told by publishers or authors. This may help explain why the *Tomorrow, When the War Began* Series has been ignored by the Children's Book Council of Australia. I guess one of the great satisfactions in life is getting the last laugh, especially as it happens so rarely. In the case of this series, Pan Macmillan and I have been laughing quite a lot.

One aspect of the book which has confused readers is that in one version it is known as *When the War Began*. This is because the publishers, Pan Macmillan, wanted to put the book out with a new jacket designed specifically to appeal to the adult market. Booksellers then complained that it would be too confusing to have the same book with the same title but two different covers. So it was decided to change the title, by dropping the word 'Tomorrow'. That meant booksellers now had a book with the same text, but two different covers and two different titles. This got them even more confused! So the idea was dropped, but it has to be said that it was a success nonetheless, because the adult edition sold out very quickly. The content of the books is completely identical, regardless of which cover or title they have.

As of January 2000, *Tomorrow, When the War Began* has been reprinted twenty-four times, and the series has sold more than a million copies. It has been published successfully in the United States and Great Britain, and been translated into Italian, Spanish, Danish, German, Swedish and Dutch. I have had forty-five approaches from film companies around the world who want to make it into a TV series, a mini series or a movie, and although I sold an option to one company, I refused their request for an extension because of communication problems with the producer and director. I was also concerned by their script, which had Kevin and Corrie engaged to each other, Kevin recast as an Aboriginal character and Chris as gay, and seemed to be drawn largely from old fashioned World War II movies starring Steve McQueen or Richard Attenborough. The series will never be filmed unless I can find someone who has a genuine commitment to maintaining its integrity.

Halfway through the novel I realised that there was too much material for just one book. I decided that I would have a go at writing a sequel, sometime in the future. The day after I finished *Tomorrow, When the War Began*, I began *The Dead of the Night*.

Chapter Eight

The Sequels to

Tomorrow, When the War Began

THE DEAD OF THE NIGHT

Moving from *Tomorrow, When the War Began* to *The Dead of the Night* was completely effortless. I was so engrossed in the situation and the characters that I couldn't wait to find out more about their futures. I wrote the second book with an intensity equal to the first.

For a long time I'd admired the 'Alex' quartet of novels by New Zealand writer Tessa Duder. The series deals with the vicissitudes of a New Zealand teenager who is a national swimming champion and eventually goes to Rome for the 1960 Olympics. The books are enormously popular in New Zealand and have a strong following in Australia too, as they richly deserve.

One of the things I liked most about the series was that the second volume, *Alex in Winter*, has a mood which is largely depressed. It's as though most of the book has a grey feeling. I thought it was brave to follow a bestseller with a sequel that felt so depressed. I'm not suggesting that I made a deliberate decision to give the same mood to *The Dead of the Night*, but I can see the influence of *Alex in Winter* on my sequel. It is logical that young people, or people of any age, having survived the initial wild adventures of a war might soon sink into a depressed and negative state. So it seemed an appropriate tone to give this particular book.

The surprising thing is that people to whom I've mentioned this invariably comment: 'But I don't think it's got that kind of mood at all!' So maybe it was in my imagination.

I liked the idea of starting with Ellie's reference to how much her previous writing had upset or angered the others. One of the fictions we enter into when reading a novel is that we are its only readers; that the characters in the story will never read it themselves. I thought it would be fun to challenge this assumption and to remind people that writing has real power, which includes the power to hurt. Honesty might be attractive to the readers of a novel, but it mightn't be as attractive to the characters in that novel.

I've always been fascinated by the power of language and the power of writing, and I refer to it quite often in my books. The ending of *Dear Miffy* is another example. It invites the reader to consider whether he or she has any right to read Tony's intimate and personal account of his life.

Of all the characters in my books, Erle in *The Great Gatenby* and Chris in the *Tomorrow* Series are the most like me when I was a teenager. Unlike Chris, about the hardest drug I've messed with is Diet Coke; but I think in my adolescence I was similar to Chris in that I tended to be alienated, not quite part of the group, and certainly inclined to write poetry, much of which was depressed. So far I haven't ended up quite as badly as Chris, but there were times when I went close.

I enjoyed creating the character of Major Harvey, who is horribly like several deputy principals whom I've met over the years. One of the ways you can make a character unattractive is to give him no sense of humour, and I did that with the Major.

Another aspect of characters in fiction that can be fascinating is a lack of self awareness. When this is taken to an extreme, the character can be either funny or monstrous. Basil Fawlty, in _Fawlty Towers_, is a good example of a comic character with no self awareness, although he is quite monstrous in some ways too. Basil seriously believes he is the best hotel manager in Europe. Everyone around him, and even the viewers at home, know he's a complete idiot. Major Harvey, in his pomposity and arrogance and weakness, has no self awareness.

Although he is sinister, I liked writing about him so much that I deliberately left open the possibility that he might have survived the explosion at the end of the book, thinking it would be fun to bring him back in a future volume.

In describing Corrie's condition in the hospital, I thought I had given a strong enough hint that she was dying, and I was a bit surprised by the number of readers who asked about her in subsequent months.

With phrases like: 'Her head on the pillow was a little black patch, an unmoving round stone . . . she was alive, yet somehow not with us any more . . . that Corrie had slipped quietly away, leaving behind this peacefully breathing, pale replacement . . .' I thought it was obvious that Corrie had moved to the next dimension, even if she had left her body in the hospital for a little longer. I really liked Corrie as a character and it was upsetting that she should die, but that was the way the story wrote itself.

The scene where Ellie slips down the cliff face is a pretty accurate description of what happened to me when I went rock climbing without ropes near Bathurst some years ago, and ended up with a severe lack of fingertips after using them to brake my slide down a vertical cliff. The scene where Fi is chased through the bush chilled me as I wrote it and chills me when I read it now. I've always thought that being followed at night by an unknown person is about as scary as life can get, so I gave it the full treatment in that chapter, and put Fi through an appalling experience. As always, my favourite scenes in the book are the intense ones: for example, Lee killing the soldier, and the death of Chris.

The title *The Dead of the Night* is supposed to be a pun, on the idea that people died during the night, and a lot of the action takes place in the middle section of the night, which is colloquially referred to as 'the dead of night', when everything is at its quietest and stillest. I'm not sure why I put the second 'the' in the title, as it was unnecessary; in fact the American publishers dropped it for their edition.

One of the immutable laws of life is that the

sequel is never as good as the original. It ranks with 'Neither a borrower nor a lender be', 'Don't trust a man who drinks alone', and 'The movie's never as good as the book'. I worked very hard to make sure that this sequel was as good as the first book in the series, and I have taken the same approach to every book since. It gives me the greatest delight when I hear people debating which of the series they like best; or when the sequels win awards. It says to me that the effort was worthwhile. The next time I see a stranger drinking by himself in a pub, I might offer to buy him a beer.

THE THIRD DAY, THE FROST

Again I approached this book with the determination that it should be as good as the first two, or at least as good as I could make it. One of the elements in my plan for all the books in the series, was that each should be as long as the others. I never wanted to become one of those writers who gets lazier as he goes along, so that the sequels get shorter and shorter.

The Third Day, the Frost and *Burning for Revenge* are my favourites of the series.

Halfway through *The Dead of the Night*, I realised that Robyn would eventually sacrifice her life for the others. It seemed consistent with her beliefs – the Christian tradition is one of martyrdom and self sac-rifice – and with her courage, nobility and grace.

This scene was emotionally the hardest thing I've ever written. I'm proud of it, and think it is the best scene in the whole series, but I was wrecked by the time I finished. I read it back many times, and never got sick of it, which makes it a unique scene for me in my own books.

I also loved writing the farm scenes, where Ellie, on the run from the enemy, cold and hungry and lost and tired, is lying in the undergrowth remembering the days before the war. One of my fondest memories of the series is reading that passage to a large audience of rural adults in Dubbo NSW some years ago. I liked the looks on their faces as they listened to this description of their own lifestyles. A kind of slow, warm pleasure seemed to spread through the hall as they heard memories of their childhoods, as well as images from their current experiences.

> *I loved the activity in the shearing shed. The sheep milling in the pens. The dogs lying in the shadows panting, their bright eyes watching the sheep, hoping they'd be called up again to run across their backs and shift them to the next yard or back to the paddock. I loved the oily feel of the classing table, the soft whiteness of the fleeces, the quiet bleating of the waiting sheep. I was proud to see our bales, with our brands on them, on the back of a truck heading for the sales. I knew they were going halfway around the world to be made into wonderful warm clothes that would be worn by city people, people I'd never meet.*

The scene in the prison again drew heavily on my experiences in Hobart after being arrested for the Franklin River demonstrations. The scene where Ellie confronts Major Harvey is a typical status battle of the kind that can be found in many books and movies. People in positions of power tend to talk slowly and loudly, using long sentences and long words. They do so because they are confident they won't be interrupted. So when Ellie finally interrupts Major Harvey, blowing all her fuses at once, the effect should be powerful, as it is when any high-status person is challenged, in real life or fiction.

> *'What's it matter to you anyway?' I screamed. 'You disgusting filthy heap of shit! What are you helping them for? You're a traitor. At least we tried. At least we did the best we could. I don't care if I do die, I'd rather be dead than end up a complete and utter arsehole like you.' I was standing and screaming, aware that little flecks of spit were flying out of my mouth and hitting his red shocked face. Not that I cared about that. Then the guards were in the room, grabbing me and throwing me onto the floor.*

I enjoyed blowing up Major Harvey. Despite the death of Robyn, it was a satisfying moment.

In casting around for a title for the book, which took months, I tried looking in a dictionary of quotations under 'third day'. The way I saw the titles working was that the war would start tomorrow, continue through the following 'night' (in effect, autumn), and then move on to the third day, the cold of winter. I was delighted to find the lines from Shakespeare's *King Henry VIII* which are quoted at the start of the book: 'The third day comes a frost, a killing frost . . .' American and British publishers used the second half of that phrase for their title, so the book is called *A Killing Frost* in those countries.

The first Australian cover was done by well-known Sydney illustrator Nick Stathopoulos. He is a specialist in, among other things, militaria, and I loved the wonderful image of the exploding ship that he put across the front and back jackets. Nevertheless, he drove me slightly crazy, because he is such a stickler for detail! At one stage it seemed like he was ringing me every night, asking questions like, 'Now, the helicopter on page 101, is that a Bell 55A, or an Excalibur Hawkeye . . .?' I would reply, 'All I know is that it's big and it flies and it's got a whirly thing on top.'

I think he found me a rather disappointing author.

The break in the barbed wire on Nick's cover is meant to represent the escape from Australia. The barbed wire is intact on the other books, to signify that Australia is a giant prison camp, with everybody (almost everybody) behind wire. So when one strand breaks, it indicates that at least some people have managed to get out.

DARKNESS, BE MY FRIEND

For a sequel to be written, two forces need to meet. One is the desire of the writer to write it; the other is the desire of the readers to read more.

With *Letters from the Inside* only one of those forces was present. I had many letters from readers requesting a sequel, and no doubt publishers would have paid plenty of money to get their hands on one. However, I had no desire to write it and at this stage still have no interest in writing it: and – as far as anyone can predict the future – I'll have no interest in ever doing so.

With the *Tomorrow* Series, however, things were a little different. Although I had planned to finish after the third book (just as I had planned to finish after the first book and then the second), the readers seemed to want more, and I certainly wanted to keep writing about these characters, who had become so much a part of my life.

So it wasn't a difficult decision to start *Darkness, Be My Friend.* And it wasn't difficult to throw Ellie and her friends back into the war zone. It was quite logical that they would be needed in Australia; that their special skills and expertise should not be wasted while the war continued to rage.

I had wanted to include more references to New Zealand in my books after making several trips there and falling in love with the country and the people. I started to realise how extraordinary it was that two countries which are so close in every sense (not only geographically, but also emotionally, culturally, politically), could have so little contact, so little knowledge and so little understanding of each other. In fact, that's not strictly true: New Zealanders probably have much more understanding of Australians than vice versa.

So it was a conscious decision to have New Zealand play a stronger role in the books, as part of a vague agenda to help make Australians more aware of this beautiful and special country.

It was also a conscious decision to have Ellie and her friends fail a number of times during this novel.

all things, I wanted to keep the series realistic. To have the group go from success to success, blowing up bigger targets each time, would become ridiculous. Failure is a part of life, and certainly a part of wars, and so it was important that even these heroes should have a downturn in their fortunes. This meant that some readers found the book unsatisfying. Many people have said to me that there is not enough action in *Darkness, Be My Friend*, although in fact they are wrong. There is as much action in the book as in the others, but the difference is that the action results in no great successes or triumphs. It's difficult to write a popular book where the characters lose, and yet it was essential if the series were to continue.

On the other hand there are a substantial number of readers who name *Darkness, Be My Friend* as their favourite in the series.

One of the scenes I most enjoyed writing was the escape from the patch of bush in the middle of the night when Ellie and the others are surrounded by enemy soldiers. It can be argued that all writing is a matter of solving problems. Who killed the murder victim? How does the boy get the girl to love him? How does the prisoner escape from the kidnappers? How does the victim reverse the magic spell? How does the woman deal with an unwanted pregnancy?

I was made very aware of this concept during the scene in the patch of bush. Having put Ellie and her friends up trees while soldiers prowl around beneath them, I then had to get them out of the situation. I was determined not to use the predictable and clichéd solutions to the problem: sneaking out quietly in the middle of the night; dressing in enemy uniforms and bluffing their way through; shooting their way out; hiding, so the enemy couldn't find them; or having a miraculous intervention from some other source (known as the _deus ex machina_ solution, which I'd already used at the end of _The Third Day, the Frost_).

For some days I worried about how to rescue them, and at one stage thought I would have to give up and rewrite the whole episode. But finally a solution occurred to me that I liked and eventually used. I was happy that it was a fresh and believable way of breaking them out of their trap.

When I wrote the book I had no idea why Iain and the other guerillas had disappeared, or where they had gone, but I thought, 'I'll worry about that when the time comes', and for several years afterwards when people asked about their fate I just made vague noises like: 'You'll find out eventually.'

The title for the book is adapted from a book called _Boldness, Be My Friend_ by Richard Pape, a true-life account of adventures in World War II that I had enjoyed as a teenager.

BURNING FOR REVENGE

Writing _Burning for Revenge_ was a blast! After the restraint of _Darkness, Be My Friend_, and the failures of the characters, it was good to be able to let rip and spend a large part of the novel describing the dramatic raid on the airport.

Using rifles to blow up fuel tanks was an idea from a tiny newspaper article that I'd read years before, about a terrorist attack on a German airfield.

My dislike of Kevin comes through most strongly in this book, where he is given such a hard time, and contributes so little to the group. Nevertheless I think it's quite credible that Kevin becomes withdrawn and depressed. He's having a full-on nervous breakdown.

The introduction of the feral children is probably inspired by *Mad Max 3*, *Lord of the Flies*, and various other sources. I did feel it was time for some new characters, as I didn't want the books to become claustrophobic, with just the same small group all the time. It seemed important to show the effect of the war on another group, young children, who would have been traumatised in all kinds of subtle and not so subtle ways by the loss of their families, their security, their education, their networks, their lifestyles.

I hadn't had to do a lot of research with these books, relying mainly on my general knowledge, as well as the occasional phone call to an expert. When writing *The Third Day, the Frost* I went to an indoor pistol range in Mount Alexander Road, Melbourne, where I found, to my surprise, that as long as I paid for an instructor to stand beside me, I could legally fire a handgun. I stood there blazing away at a target, not really enjoying it, but carefully noting details like the quantity of smoke, the way the empty shell ejected, the amount of recoil.

But I did do some vital research for *Burning for Revenge*. Ellie recalls how she and Fi microwaved an Easter egg. I can't remember why I wanted to write such a sequence into the novel, but to make sure it was authentic I got an Easter egg, put it in my own microwave and turned it to 'High'. The result was as described in the book: 'the most disgusting black toxic-looking liquid. It filled the kitchen with smoke, and a smell that didn't go away for hours.'

As a writer you have to suffer for your art.

THE NIGHT IS FOR HUNTING

With each book, the popularity of the series grew and the pressure on me increased. I didn't mind it; in fact, quite the opposite, I loved it and appreciated it and was very moved by the reactions of readers. But it made it all the more important to maintain the standard, and I became especially aware of that as the end of the series approached.

Halfway through *Burning for Revenge* I sat back and looked at the series as a whole, and the direction in which it was heading, and came to the realisation that it would be better to finish it too soon rather than too late. Comedians are always told to leave the audience laughing. In other words, don't go on for so long that the audience are yawning and looking at their watches; better to get off the stage while the audience still want more, as then they'll probably turn up for your next gig.

I wanted to finish the series early rather than late because I was worried that if I started running out of ideas and energy readers would be quick to notice and would feel disappointed.

I had plenty of ideas and energy for a couple of books yet. I knew I had too much stuff to fit into just one more book and to capture the whole tapestry of the war I felt that one book would be insufficient. So

I made the decision to stop at seven, and from then on the tempo of the books was adapted accordingly.

I'd also been conscious of the need not to age the characters too much. The Billabong series, which had meant so much to me as a child, had certainly gone on too long. The characters aged so much that they didn't hold their interest for me and most other readers. By the end of the series the characters, who were thirteen or fourteen when we first met them, were middle-aged adults with children of their own. As a kid I found them boring.

In the *Tomorrow* Series I aged my characters as gradually as I could. The whole span of the war is only fifteen months, so the characters, who in my mind were at the start of Year 12 when *Tomorrow, When the War Began* opens, are seventeen or eighteen by the end of the last book. However, although they don't age much in chronological terms, they obviously have to mature and age in other ways, if only as a result of the experiences they endure.

What I wanted to do in *The Night is for Hunting* was to have them evolve to the next stage of their development. They had already gone from being teenagers to young adults; now it was time for them to become parents. However, I didn't want Ellie to give birth to triplets or for any of the characters to become parents literally, so it had to be done in a more subtle and metaphorical sense. Hence the role of the 'feral' kids in the sixth book. I enjoyed writing these kids into the book, and imagining the kind of existence they would have led, and I felt they were a sympathetic and interesting group.

Over the years many people have asked me to

write books about many topics, usually about some issue or minority group in which they have their own interest. I've never pursued any of these suggestions, because their interests haven't accorded with mine. But one night at a function in the Ringwood area of Melbourne a woman approached me after I'd given a talk. She explained that she was a teacher or teacher's aide working with deaf children, and told me how impossible it was to find books with deaf characters for the children to read. She said the students were delighted whenever they did find a book with a deaf person in it, no matter what the age, gender or personality of the character. She asked me if I could put a deaf character into one of my books, and told me it would mean a great deal to her students.

I was moved by her description of her students, and so Gavin became the first character in any of my books to have been influenced by such a suggestion from a reader.

One of my favourite pieces of literature is a few pages from a nineteenth-century Australian classic called *Such is Life*, by Joseph Furphy. In a sequence which has been described as the best short story in Australian literature (it is in fact part of a chapter of the book, but it is a self-contained episode, and so in a sense could be called a short story) Furphy tells the terrible and tragic tale of a child lost in the bush and the desperate search that ensues. It is one of the most poignant and relentless pieces of writing I have experienced, and I'm sure it influenced me in writing the sequence where Ellie and the others go searching for the missing feral children.

I also thought it was important to vary the tone of

the series again, and to step out of the war for a while. Endless pages of gunfights and explosions would be as wearying for the reader as for the writer, and so in this bush sequence we can virtually forget the war and enter a different drama.

The Christmas scene also arose out of a desire to provide contrast, and to give the characters and readers a sense that positive, creative and life-affirming events can still occur, even in the middle of a war. When Ellie and the others start their school, they are not only implying that life can go on, they are taking their roles and responsibilities as parents more seriously and more effectively.

The school gives a chance to show other aspects of the characters, and gives a chance to rehabilitate Kevin to some extent, and to show that he still has his own strengths.

For the first time, I used a 'Saturday matinee serial ending' for this book, because I thought it would make a change from the others. It would have been all too easy to end each book with a death, but I didn't want the predictability and repetition of that, and I also wanted to have a few characters left alive for the last book in the series. If I'd killed one of them off in each book there wouldn't have been many left standing by *The Other Side of Dawn*.

For the first time in the series there is a full-on gun battle in *The Night is for Hunting*. It was time to use such a scene, as with the war becoming more advanced, and the teenagers becoming more proficient as soldiers, they could be expected to hold their own in the country around Tailor's Stitch which was so familiar to them.

THE OTHER SIDE OF DAWN

I started the seventh and last book in the series feeling huge pressure. However I always knew there was plenty more to write about, that I would never run out of material for this group of characters in this situation, so I wasn't too worried about the content of the book. In fact, one of my main priorities was a little strange: I was determined to make this the longest of the series, mainly to end on a high note, but also because I still wanted readers to know they were not being short changed. I didn't want the series to fizzle out, or for me to be lazy – in other words, to take the money and run!

The cliffhanger ending to the sixth book meant I had no difficulty starting the seventh, and a couple of storylines were already in the back of my mind. I've always thought scenes on trains are very exciting in movies, so I thought it would be good to have one in a book, and I wanted Ellie to be on her own for a period of time.

A book called *The Phantom Major*, by Virginia Cowles, tells the true story of Major David Stirling, a British Army officer in North Africa during World War II. Stirling formed a specialist unit to engage in guerilla warfare behind enemy lines. They were called the Special Air Services, better known as the SAS, and they survive under that name to this day. When reading this book I was impressed by the way Stirling's troops operated, hitting airfield after airfield, petrol dump after petrol dump, enemy barracks after enemy barracks, causing great damage with comparatively little loss to themselves. They did so much damage that I could never have convinced readers in a work of fiction that such achievements were possible. I guess in real life people do get slack and unobservant, even when their lives are on the line, and it seemed that many of the German soldiers guarding air bases must have been half asleep most of the time.

Anyway, that was the main sense I wanted in *The Other Side of Dawn*. I thought it would be good to have Ellie and the others travel light, strike hard and often, and do maximum damage.

As so often happens, however, the book took control, and they ended up attempting only one major raid.

I originally wrote the book in such a way that after each intense scene there was a chapter or two where Ellie and the group relaxed and took it easy. So in the first draft the time spent in Stratton dragged on for some weeks while they waited for the green light from Ryan. And Ellie's prisoner of war camp was quite humane and civilised. However, the three people from Pan Macmillan who read the first draft were unanimous in wanting those scenes made tougher, with more tension and suffering. So I set about doing some major rewrites. In fact I did more rewrites for this book than for any other in the series, and for the first time in my writing career I missed a publisher's deadline – only by a couple of weeks, but I was embarrassed about it.

The other big change that occurred after the first draft was the removal of a baby from the book. Danielle Sloper – a Queensland teenager I was talking to after a workshop – suggested it would add dramatic tension if Ellie found her mother had been raped by the soldiers.

I went away thinking it would be even better if her mother had not only been raped but had a baby. I thought this would add a powerful new dimension to the story, as well as emphasising the kind of atrocities that happen so frequently in wars. So I wrote it that way. But again the three readers at Pan Macmillan were unanimous in saying the baby was an annoying and unnecessary addition to the story, and there wasn't time or room in one book to fully explore the implications of Ellie having an unwanted baby brother. So during one of the rewrites the baby disappeared.

Judy, the Australian woman who runs the prison camp, is based on Mrs Judy McCowan, a respected colleague with whom I worked at Geelong Grammar School. The headmistress who makes only a brief appearance in *So Much to Tell You* is also based on Judy McCowan. I guess she must have made a strong impact on me to appear in two different books in two different guises.

Ellie's description of her house, coming at the end of the seventh book, is based strongly on the property where I now live, the Tye Estate, near Romsey in Victoria. Each feature which Ellie describes can be found in and around my house:

> *From here I can see the old fountain, where there used to be a statue of a lady with an umbrella, before someone vandalised her during the war. I can see the white bridge over the creek, the fake stone goanna at the foot of the gum tree, the carport with the grapevine growing over it, the flat stretch of grass leading to the little waterfall, the Japanese maple and the old barn and the*

Dumpmaster and the rows of hydrangeas and the
duck dam with its stone bridge and little island
and wire arch of wisteria . . .

I used this property in even more detail as the setting for my next book, *Winter*.

As usual I put in a few private jokes. One of them is where Ellie quotes a line from *So Much to Tell You,* and mentions that it's from some book she's read, but she can't remember its name. The other is the reference to Ellie's great-grandmother Tommy. For the first time, Ellie is given a surname in this book. The choice of surnames and the reference to Tommy are meant to hint that Ellie is the great-granddaughter of Jim and Tommy Linton. Jim is the brother of Norah, the heroine of the Billabong series. Norah was resourceful, brave, loving and could act with initiative and maturity when required. These seem like appropriate qualities for Ellie's ancestors. But by hinting that Ellie is related to the Lintons of Billabong, I wanted also to show my respect for Mary Grant Bruce's books. There are many parallels between the two series, not the least being that both of them contain many volumes. Both of them have been popular with the generations for whom they were written; both involve young Australians living on farm properties; both show young Australians battling 'the baddies' and winning.

I deliberately gave the first book in the series, *Tomorrow, When the War Began,* an old-fashioned feel when I was writing it, to evoke memories of earlier books like those of Mary Grant Bruce and Joan Phipson. I had the Billabong series strongly in mind from the day I started writing *Tomorrow, When the War Began.*

So at last the time came when I was able to put down the pen – or turn off the computer – knowing this series was ended.

And then I started to feel even more pressure. As the build-up to the book's publication intensified I started to realise how much was riding on *The Other Side of Dawn*. Adults and teenagers told me, in every imaginable way, just how much they expected of this book. On 28 September 1999, the day of its release, I downloaded some emails, at about six p.m., and there it was – the first reader's first reaction. It came from Lisa Caswell, a student in Hobart, and it was overwhelmingly positive and generous.

Over the next twenty-four hours I received another dozen. They were all extremely positive, except for one future English teacher who wrote: 'If you were trying to spell Malaysia on page 81, you got it wrong.'

As I'd been trying to spell Malaya, not Malaysia, I ignored his message.

But opening these first dozen messages, feeling sick with nerves as I read each one, I realised that, yes, the pressure had definitely got to me.

Writing the series absorbed many years of my life. But I have never regretted it for a moment. It's been a wonderful adventure, not just in the creation and writing of each book, not just in empathising with the characters and feeling that I was sharing their experiences, but in listening to the responses of readers. I did, as I have said, expect the books to be a hit, but the time came, somewhere in early 1999, when I realised that their success had exceeded all my expectations, and I had to sit back and think 'My God, this really has gone beyond my wildest dreams.'

I received so many moving comments, letters and emails about the books that I had tears in my eyes many times. Perhaps it is best, as I have done before, to let someone else sum up the experience. Many of the letters from readers commented on the fact that Ellie's courage inspired them to be braver in their own daily lives. I particularly treasured this one, from Katy Parsons of Moss Vale, NSW, who wrote: 'when Ellie talks (or writes) about her perspective of life, I realise how alike her and I are; we think a lot about how cruel or how kind, how strange or how clear things in life are. And she makes me think about life in odd and beautiful ways. These teenagers have given me confidence to do really wild things.' Katy then described how she took over a school assembly and ran it when she felt it wasn't being done properly. She continued: 'when I reached my classroom and sat down, I was shaking so much. Before I read these books, I wouldn't have even been able to go as far as touch the microphone, let alone talk into one.'

It seems appropriate to let a reader have the last word.

Chapter Nine

Checkers

In a hypothetical Australian state, a hypothetical premier has some hypothetical rich mates. When a hypothetical casino licence – in effect a licence to print money – is up for grabs, it is his hypothetical rich mates who get the contract.

It would be illegal in any Australian state for a premier to favour his own friends in such a situation. Such public contracts have to be available on equal terms to all applicants.

In many countries political novels are popular, and there is a long tradition of them, but not in Australia. There have been very few political novels in this country; although I remember reading one as a teenager. It was called *McCabe, P.M.*, by John Rowe.

Another situation that intrigues me, and which I had already explored in *Looking for Trouble*, is the effect on children of dishonest parents. What do you do if your father gets arrested? Especially if you have always believed him to be a man of integrity. Or if you have believed him to be capable and infallible.

In my teaching career I came across a number of students in such a situation, and I felt some of their pain as they struggled to come to terms with the frightening and devastating directions their lives had taken, through no fault of their own. One of the most powerful forces in most children's lives is the belief that their parents are Superman and Superwoman, and to have this belief damaged or shattered at too early an age can be traumatic.

I was also interested in revisiting the world of the psychiatric ward, which has always been a fertile ground for writers and which holds a particular fascination for me. This is partly a result of my own life experiences; but also because the failure of masks, and the revelation of the real people behind them, which is particularly evident in psych wards.

For some time I had in my head the voice of an adolescent girl in such a situation, and although I could just hear her in my brain, I couldn't get the voice on paper. I made a number of attempts, and finally one night in a motel in Goulburn I wrote half a page and thought: 'Yes, that's it!'

At that stage I didn't have a plot or much idea of what would happen; but, once again, having got the voice, I was confident the rest would follow. And so the nameless character's life began to take shape. It turned out she had a mother who was obsessed with keeping the house clean (in itself a sign of mental instability), a father who was both weak and strong (weak in his relationship with his boss, but giving an appearance of strength in his relationship with his family), a younger brother who was already heading down the same path as his father, and a dog called Checkers.

The name Checkers, and indeed the idea for using a dog as a plot device, came from a true story. In 1956 Richard Nixon was a candidate for Vice President of the United States, on the same ticket as the popular President Eisenhower. But Nixon's chances were severely jeopardised by accusations that he took illegal donations from supporters. Nixon was about to be dumped by Eisenhower, but he had one last chance to keep his place. He went on television and addressed the American nation. He denied any wrongdoing, denied taking bribes, denied accepting illegal gifts. 'However,' he said, as his wife Patricia sat nervously beside him, 'there is one exception. We did accept a gift of a dog from a contributor. The dog has become very special to my children, and no matter how much the American people might want us to return the dog, we are not going to.'

He spoke about the dog so sentimentally that by the time he'd finished there wasn't a dry eye left in an American household, and Nixon survived as Eisenhower's running mate. They went on to win the election, and Nixon became Vice President. In 1960 Nixon ran for President and lost narrowly to John Kennedy. But in 1968 he ran again and this time won. The rest is history. Nixon was later revealed as one of the most dishonest and corrupt people ever to occupy the White House, and was forced to resign in disgrace. Perhaps if he'd not been able to use his dog so movingly and effectively back in 1956, America and the world would be a better place today.

The dog's name was Checkers.

I've always loved reading animal stories, and although *Checkers* could not really be described as an animal story, I did very much enjoy writing about the dog. He is based quite strongly on the dog I owned at the time, a mongrel from the Lost Dogs' Home. He was a cross between a springer-spaniel and a border-collie, and he had a black and white coat. I named him Albie, and he was the biggest dag I've ever seen. Many of the episodes involving Checkers that I've described in the book were taken from incidents with Albie.

Albie loved walks, and at one stage when I offered to take him on a walk he sprang at the front door so enthusiastically that he seemed not to notice the open trap door in front of it. He took a flying leap and disappeared straight down the black hole that dropped two metres into the cellar. As usual he was not injured, but getting him back up the ladder was quite a problem.

He seemed indestructible. At one stage, just as described in the book, he ran between a car and a trailer, hardly seeming to notice they were there, even though they were travelling at high speed, and I still cannot understand how he timed the leap so perfectly that he was uninjured. Another time he was not so lucky, and a car hit him. Again the car was travelling pretty fast and I thought Albie had been killed, but he jumped up again, looking a bit shocked, trotted into the garden, and sat under a tree for a couple of hours until he felt OK.

Perhaps my worst moment with Albie came when he tried to jump a barbed wire fence while pursuing a rabbit. Unfortunately he didn't quite make it. The first I knew was when I heard a terrified yelping and screaming. I looked around and there was Albie hanging from the top of the fence. I ran over at full speed to save him, but it was not until I got there that I realised he was actually hanging by his penis, which had been caught in a barb of the wire. Only then could I truly understand the depth of feeling behind his yelps. I lifted him off carefully – very carefully – and put him on the ground, where he shook himself and raced off after another rabbit, with no apparent damage except a drop of blood on his sheath.

Even thinking about it now makes my eyes water.

I had real tears on the day Albie died. I'd taken him to the vet, because after returning from a long trip I found he'd lost a lot of weight and seemed listless and ill. It turned out that he had massive cancer beginning in his kidneys but spreading through his system. The vet put him to sleep rather than bring him back after the operation. I don't think I've ever wept as much in my life as I did that day.

So it was good to be able to commemorate Albie in the book, although I was a little disconcerted when a woman in Adelaide opened *Checkers*, looked at the dedication, and said: 'Don't tell me you've dedicated this book to a dead dog!'

I enjoyed recreating the world of the adolescent psychiatric ward, with its gallery of sensitive and highly strung characters, all suffering pain in different ways. And I enjoyed recreating the identities of different staff members, mostly based on people I'd met over the years, but again drawn largely from the imagination. The decision not to give the narrator a name was done with the same intent as in *So Much to*

Tell You. In *So Much to Tell You* Marina does get her name on the last page of the book, signifying that she has come far enough on her journey to be able to take on a sense of identity again. It's like a christening, or baptism. But the girl in *Checkers* has not travelled quite so far. She has lost her family, her friends, her confidence, and like so many of the characters in my books, she has pretty much lost her voice. She is getting better but she still has some way to go.

As the book was about to be published I finished writing my next novel, *Dear Miffy*, and I realised that there was a great opportunity for another private joke. So I grabbed the proofs back from the printer at the last moment, and inserted a sentence which suggests that the girl in *Checkers* meets Tony from *Dear Miffy* in the psychiatric ward. 'There's Tony, who's in a wheelchair, but he's meant to be really violent.' That enabled me to go back to *Dear Miffy* and insert a similar reference in that:

> *There's this girl here, reminds me of you a bit,*
> *Miff, talks like you, posh accent and all that.*
> *When she does talk, which is about once a week.*
> *We've got that in common. She's nice looking but I*
> *don't think she's going to be dropping round to see*
> *me too often.*

He goes on to describe her father as 'real rich' and 'real famous'.

A few clever readers have picked up the connection between the two books, but it's only obvious to people who read pretty closely.

Some readers find the novel difficult, because of

the political and financial content. It certainly gets quite complicated, but it doesn't really matter whether people understand the technical language as long as they get the general idea, and as long as they are not too alienated by that information. Of all my books, *Checkers* and *Looking for Trouble* remain my favourites. One of the greatest compliments I've ever had was for *Checkers*, when a friend in Melbourne, a psychologist employed by the adolescent unit of a private psychiatric hospital, got her patients to read the book as a group. They took it in turns, each reading aloud to the rest of the group until they'd finished. At that point one of them turned to my friend and said: 'Has he been eavesdropping on us? Have you been taping us secretly? How come he knows so much about us?'

That unsolicited testimonial to the authenticity of the book moved me deeply and made me proud to have written it. The pain of children and adolescents in situations like theirs, so often not of their own making, is an area in which we as a society have much to do before we can truly say we look after our young people.

Chapter Ten

Dear Miffy

There's a popular theory, much loved by tabloid news-papers and shallow current-affairs programmes on TV, that if you take a young person who's been doing drugs or getting into crime or living as a street kid, and put him into a nice loving family for a couple of days, or send him to the country to milk cows and breathe fresh air, he'll be all fixed up and will live hap-pily ever after. It's like, no matter how big or serious the problems, a bit of love will fix it.

Strangely enough it can occasionally happen more or less that way. I had a letter from a reader in Perth, who didn't enclose a surname or return address, but who told me how she'd been in hospital after a suicide attempt. When she'd recovered con-sciousness her parents were standing by the bed, and all they kept saying was: 'How could you do this to us?'

She stayed in hospital for weeks, still depressed,

with no interest in living. One day, however, a nurse said to her: 'You are a wonderful person with so many talents. Don't do this to yourself.'

She told me how that was the turning point in her life, and for years afterwards as she struggled to get things together, it was that kind comment by a virtual stranger that kept her going.

Nevertheless, I'm not a big fan of the idea that massive problems can be solved by simple solutions. I suppose the belief that life is complex and subtle has underpinned much of my writing, and it was certainly strongly present during *Dear Miffy*.

I reread the book before writing this chapter and was satisfied with it. I didn't quite know what to expect, because I hadn't looked at it for a long time. In fact, with all of my books I go through the same sequence: I write them, read them for errors, read them again maybe a couple of times, making various alterations, then send them to the editor. When the editor comes back with her suggestions I go through the manuscript again, making more changes. Later, when the proofs come from the printer, I read it again, looking for any last minute mistakes that need to be fixed. When the book is published and I hold the first copy in my hands, the feeling is wonderful, euphoric. To celebrate I keep the book briefly for some days or weeks and keep looking at it. During this period I might read it again, maybe twice. Then suddenly I'm sick of it and from that time on I never open it unless I have to find an answer to a question a reader has asked, or check some fact for accuracy.

So rereading any of my titles for this book now, including *Dear Miffy*, took an act of will, and with all of them I was a little curious and apprehensive as to what I would find.

Of course with *Dear Miffy* I was especially apprehensive because of its controversial nature and the strong responses people had to it. When you include so much swearing in a book for young people, along with sex, violence and a bleak ending, you have to expect some controversy, so little of it surprised me much, although I was staggered to hear of bookshops refusing to stock the book. It seems amazing that anyone could be so arrogant as to take it upon himself or herself to decide what the people in the suburb will be allowed to read.

Occasionally the reactions became quite extreme. At one school a male teacher was so angry about the book that I thought he might hit me. As he abused me in a long raging tirade I realised why he didn't like *Dear Miffy*. It was because he recognised his own violence in the book, and it made him uncomfortable.

For a long time I had wanted to write a book that was genuinely in the voice of an Australian teenager. It's always been a convention in fiction that characters are not given the same voices they have in real life. For example, in real life we insert lots of 'ums' and 'ahs' in our speech, we repeat ourselves, and we meander. In fiction it would be incredibly boring if characters did that, so in virtually all fiction the characters talk in structured and purposeful language.

In writing for young people, authors have always avoided the swear words that most teenagers use. It's interesting going into schools and asking teenagers if there is anyone in their age group who doesn't swear. Sometimes, amid much laughter, they'll nominate one or two students in the class, who then usually deny indignantly that they don't swear. 'But I did swear just the other day!' Rarely, one of them will agree they don't swear. I respect people who have such strength of mind during their teenage years, but nevertheless the fact remains that most teenagers swear a lot. And yet that's never properly reflected in books.

There's also far more personal abuse, and sexist and racist exchanges between most teenagers than normally appear in fiction. Often it's almost friendly, and indeed it can even be part of the flirting process, but it makes adults edgy and upset.

So it was quite satisfying to have a character use a voice that was authentic for a certain subculture of Australian youth.

This particular subculture is one that has not been written about often in Australia. It's the subculture of some young men and women from tough suburbs in big cities, who dress and act and talk in a way that people from more conservative areas find deeply threatening. Frankly, I find them pretty threatening. If I'm on a train and a group of young men burst into the carriage, shoving each other around, spitting, swearing, playing loud music, yelling, then I dive under the seat and stay there until they're gone.

But, as with most of my books, *Dear Miffy* is about understanding. Understanding people I don't understand very well. When I read about someone who bashes up a pensioner and steals their handbag, or someone who chisels off Aboriginal rock art that has been there for thousands of years, or someone who writes racist graffiti on walls, then like most people I feel deeply disturbed and upset. But I also want to understand why this happens. I want to know the mindset of someone who thinks and behaves in these ways. I want to know what the voice in their own heads is telling them.

So I did that through the character of Tony.

Tony is a character for whom I have a lot of sympathy, even though he is pretty appalling. Tony's biggest problem is that like Major Harvey he has no self awareness, no insight. He never realises that his biggest problem is himself. A lot of things that have happened to him are terrible, but the solutions lie in his hands. He needs to recognise that he truly is violent; that he truly is quite horrifying. Until he recognises these dire aspects of himself he won't get anywhere. After stabbing his father's girlfriend he writes: 'I was grounded something bad. I couldn't see why really. I mean, it's not like I was some uncontrollable maniac who was going to go around the streets killing people.'

He seems to think that stabbing someone is roughly equivalent to having overdue library books, or firing a spitball at a friend in class.

Even when people try to help him, Tony can't recognise it. When his old teacher visits him in the centre where Tony is now contained, Tony refuses to acknowledge what a kind and supportive act this is. To him, all adults, and especially authority figures, are as corrupt as himself.

It's not surprising that he should feel this way after the experiences of his life, but if he is going to make any progress, he has to unlearn those attitudes and see the world in its true colours.

I do like the relationship Tony has with Miffy though. I like her and I like the way they get along together. Tony and Miffy are so real to me that when I reread the book I could see them both clearly. It's always fun to write about people of different backgrounds having a romance. I did it in *The Great Gatenby*, although Erle and Melanie are closer in status than Tony and Miffy.

It's also fun to write about a relationship where hate turns to love. It happens quite often in real life, and it's as fascinating then as it is in fiction. In *Looking for Trouble* there was a hint of it in a primary-school romance, where a boy and girl who hate each other end up going together for a while.

One of the incidents that sparked me to write *Dear Miffy* was seeing a photograph in a newspaper of a young man who had attempted suicide. He had been locked up in a police cell – I think he was drunk at the time – and had hanged himself there, but was found and cut down while still alive. The tragic and horrifying consequence was that he suffered permanent irreversible brain damage and was condemned to be a virtual vegetable for the rest of his life. The photograph haunted me, and one of the things that made it unforgettable was my realisation that anyone who seriously contemplated committing suicide would never think of such a scenario. You think that either you are going to die in the next few minutes or hours, or that it will go wrong and you will survive. I doubt if anyone in that position truly considers they might do neither, but might instead give themselves brain damage, or damage their body so terribly that although they will live for another sixty or seventy years, they will be for ever disabled because of the depression they suffered at the age of sixteen or eighteen or twenty.

I didn't want to write some moralistic, cautionary tale warning against suicide; I wanted to write about a real person, and explore and understand his life. But it would please me very much if I thought the book made anyone resile from thoughts of suicide.

It is sometimes argued that books about suicide encourage suicide attempts by young people, and I certainly got a few letters suggesting passionately that *Dear Miffy* would have such an influence. A prominent psychiatrist suggested something similar to me. I cannot believe it, and I think on this occasion that the prominent psychiatrist got it wrong. I suppose being a prominent psychiatrist doesn't make you infallible. To me, *Dear Miffy* is the most anti-suicide book ever written. The idea that young people are so impressionable that one book can convince them to commit suicide is insulting to young people. Being impressionable is a function of personality and experience, not age.

The last paragraph of the book is meant to make people reflect upon the nature of reading. Why do we read fiction? Is it just to escape, as a lot of people suggest, or are there more complex motivations? I think one of the reasons we read is voyeuristic. We are fascinated by other people's lives, we want to explore intimately their thoughts, their feelings, their sexuality, their actions. We can't often do it in real life, although we try hard enough. But in fiction there are no limits. No-one steps in front of us and says, 'I don't think this is any of your business', or 'I refuse to answer that question'. No-one pulls down blinds. So it is quite exciting, and often quite satisfying, to be able to explore the innermost rooms of people's lives, with the author as our guide. Tony's final outburst in *Dear Miffy* is ostensibly aimed at the staff in the institution, who are frustrating him by their constant supervision and involvement; but it is really aimed at you, the reader. It is asking: 'Do you have different rights in fiction to the rights you have in real life? Is there something unhealthy about the act of reading fiction?'

Of course, in confronting readers with this question, I am neatly avoiding looking at the role of the author – the guide in these voyeuristic wanderings. If it is wrong for the reader to explore other people's lives so intimately, then where does that leave the person who conducts the tour?

Chapter Eleven

Winter

In January 1998 a major change took place in my life, when I moved to the Tye Estate on the outskirts of Melbourne.

I'd been looking for a long time to find somewhere to live, and where I could at the same time run writing courses extending over a number of days. I felt this would be much more satisfying than 'hit and run' workshops, and I had enjoyed writing camps organised by other schools, notably Hamilton College in Victoria.

I wanted a big property in a beautiful setting with good accommodation standards and close to Melbourne, and I looked at a number of places, particularly in the Mount Macedon area. One mansion on the top of Mount Macedon had previously been a guesthouse, and was owned by a Swiss couple who had led fascinating lives. The man had been Sir Winston Churchill's personal valet during and after World War II, and the guesthouse had seen many famous visitors during the 1960s and 70s. It had a magnificent garden, but the building itself needed quite a lot of internal work to bring it up to a good standard again. There was an additional problem in that it didn't have enough space for large groups of people. Nevertheless I made an offer to buy the house. My offer was rejected and I was contemplating making a higher offer when I saw an advertisement for the Tye Estate.

I was on a plane to Darwin at the time, and couldn't wait to ring the agent, so called him on my mobile phone from Darwin Airport. The young man I spoke to wasn't particularly enthusiastic about the property, and the way he described it made me feel that it wouldn't be worth my time to go and look at it. However, later I spoke to another agent, who knew more exactly the kind of place I wanted, and he said he thought it would be worth my while to check it out.

Within twenty minutes of entering the property I had decided to buy it. The Tye Estate comprises 850 acres of bush and, remarkably, it is bush in original condition. Through an historical fluke no European weeds have invaded the property (except in a few cleared areas) because no cattle or sheep have grazed it. It is full of kangaroos, wallabies, koalas, platypuses, bandicoots, and echidnas and is believed to be home to highly endangered species like powerful owls and tiger quolls. As well it had an attractive old house which was shabby and unloved, but which I thought would restore quite well, and fantastic accommodation for groups of up to thirty-two people. It also had the best classroom I'd ever seen.

So I bought the property and moved in, and never stopped loving it from the day I arrived. The old house

did need quite a bit of work, but I waited patiently
while it was done. I had the carpet torn up and thrown
out and the beautiful Baltic pine underneath sanded
and polished. I had telephone lines, power points, a
security system, ducted heating, extra lighting and
even a dishwasher installed, and then had the place
painted inside and out. By the time curtains were
hung I found myself living in the most beautiful home
I had ever owned. It was an exciting experience to see
something restored from such a plain and unattractive
condition to a house that glows with life and beauty. At
the same time there was some disappointment. Many
people in the district told me about the beautiful old
furniture which the Tye family had left in the house,
but which had since mysteriously disappeared.

The property had been owned by the Tye family for
fifty years, but upon the death of Allen and Cecilia Tye
it was bequeathed to blind and deaf Victorians, to be
used for their recreation and education. Along with
the huge property and buildings, Allen and Cecilia Tye
left their entire fortune for the running of the place.
For fifty years members of the blind and deaf community used the property frequently, during which it was
run by a trust, who appointed various managers to look
after it. Unfortunately the money eventually ran out;
hence the sale of the property to me in late 1997.

On a number of occasions after finishing the seventh book in the *Tomorrow* Series I had started writing
other books, but each time I stopped within a few pages,
feeling that something wasn't working. I began to get
nervous that maybe I'd never be able to write another
book; that the *Tomorrow* Series was my swansong.

One day, however, I thought of an opening line

which might fit one of the stories that was floating around in my head. The line was: 'I came home when I was sixteen.' I jotted it down on the back of an envelope, and a couple of days later thought, 'I must find that envelope, and put the sentence into the computer and see what happens'. So I did exactly that: typed out the opening sentence, then another sentence, then another and in record time – fifteen days to be exact – I had finished a 30,000-word novel.

I have never enjoyed writing a novel more. I was totally in love with Winter, as a character and as a book, and couldn't wait to get back to the computer every time I had a spare moment. I think the experience of buying this property and gradually restoring it to full health – not just the buildings, but the grounds as well – was such a satisfying and exhilarating experience that it translated easily into fiction.

The storyline came from that, as well as my sadness at seeing some of the neglected areas around the property, and my determination to remedy that neglect. So when Winter checks gutters, or agonizes over trees cut down, or pulls out blackberries, she is going through the emotions and experiences that I had, either on this property, or in other places where I have lived.

Some years ago I wrote a short story for an American anthology, about a girl trying to find out how her mother had died. The story was not used, but the idea stayed in my head for a long time, and I was happy to be able to explore it more fully in this book. This is a detective story in a sense, like *So Much to Tell You* and *Letters from the Inside*, and it is probably influenced by my love of Agatha Christie novels when I was in primary and secondary schools.

Orphans have always been a subject of fascination for writers, in books ranging from *Anne of Green Gables* to *The Great Gilly Hopkins*. In older books orphans are usually presented in sentimental and romantic terms. I haven't met many young orphans in my life, but the ones I have met have not seen anything romantic or attractive in their situation. There is nothing mushy about Winter, nor is she a sentimentalist. She is perhaps the strongest character I've written, in the sense that she has tremendous determination and is able to assert herself against all kinds of opposition.

It struck me as I was finishing the story that this was a real 'girl power' book.

The setting for *Winter* is the Tye Estate. The book is an accurate description of the property, except for the logging operations performed illegally and discovered by Winter on her way to the lookout. The house itself, and the various gullies, bridges and gardens described in the book are drawn from real life.

Finally, a word about Winter's name. I love poetic names. One of my favorite books, when I was a teenager, was about a girl whose given name was Gentle, which at the time I thought was wonderful, but which nowadays I don't find so attractive. But names like Rebel, River and Willow have always struck me as great choices. So when a student named Winter came to one of my writing camps, I was instantly attracted to the name, and thought then that I would love to use it in a story. Rather to my own surprise it was only a couple of months later that I began writing that book.

A Final Word

For many years I dreamed of having a book published, dreamed of people reading such a book, dreamed of people responding to it. For the dream to come true has been the most remarkable event of my life, and I'm still coming to terms with it. In an obvious way it has brought many benefits: I've been able to travel to places I could never have expected to visit, meet people I could never have expected to meet, make a good income, and receive wonderful feedback that has often moved me greatly. But more deeply than that, it has given me confidence, and helped me to understand myself better, and for that alone I am deeply grateful to books, and more importantly, to the readers who have supported me so strongly during this time. I hope to find more stories yet that will engage my interest and more situations that I want to explore through the extraordinary and powerful medium of fiction.

Coming soon from Pan Macmillan

John Marsden
Winter

'I came home when I was sixteen.'

Winter has been away a long time. Mystery surrounded her departure, and mystery surrounds her return.

Winter has come home to find answers. Her past is confused, muddled, almost lost.

Somehow she has to find that past. Somehow she has to make sense of it. If there is to be hope in her future, Winter must find the answer to the greatest question in her life.

John Marsden is known for his depiction of strong female characters, like Tracey and Mandy in *Letters from the Inside*, Marina and Lisa in *So Much to Tell You* and *Take My Word for It,* and Ellie in the *Tomorrow* Series.

But Winter de Salis is the strongest character that John Marsden has ever written.

Winter is an intense, emotionally rich book that you will want to read not just once, but many times.

To be released in 2000, *Winter* is John Marsden's first fiction book since the end of the *Tomorrow, When the War Began* Series.

John Marsden
Take My Word for It

*You know what Tracey said to me after English
today? She said: 'The reason you've got no friends is
that you don't tell anyone your problems'...I hate the
way they tell everyone every single detail about
themselves...If you ask me, it's dangerous. Once
you start, you don't stop.*

Strong, cold, private...this is Lisa, as seen by
Marina in her journal, *So Much to Tell You*.

But Lisa too keeps a journal. It's a record of her
friends and family, her frustrations and successes,
her thoughts and feelings. As page follows page, the
real Lisa begins to emerge. Not always strong, not
always private and certainly not cold.

As in the best-selling *So Much to Tell You*, award-
winning novelist John Marsden takes us into the
world of young people trying to make sense of
their lives.

'This is a deeply moving novel, beautifully crafted
and leading avid readers to anticipate more'
CANBERRA TIMES

'John Marsden has made an art form out of the
language of young adults'
THE AGE

John Marsden
The Great Gatenby

Maybe deep down every kid knows his parents want
him to be the Pride of the School, the Captain of the
Cricket and Tennis and Rowing and Darts and
Knitting and anything else that's going down.

They don't want to know that you've had more
detentions than any other new student in the history
of the school, that you're going out with a girl who
doesn't wear a bra to PE, and that the Head
Swimming Coach is some kind of Nazi whose last job
was training the shark in *Jaws*.

Erle Gatenby has been sent to boarding school to
straighten out, but there's about as much chance of
that happening as there is of his giving up
smoking ... or drinking ... or falling through the
Art Room roof.

Erle's a full tank of petrol and wild, sexy Melanie
Tozer is about to light the match.

John Marsden
The Journey

By the author of *So Much To Tell You*, *The Journey* is
a story of young people in a world so different and
yet so like our own. It is a world in which young
people must undertake a journey of discovery on
their way to becoming adults.

Argus sets out on his journey away from his valley
and his parents, never knowing what adventure will
befall him next. He learns how to survive in the wild
until he meets with a travelling fair, which he joins,
becoming a friend of Mayon the storyteller, of Lavolta
and Parara—twins who share the same body—and
many others.

But it is with the sweet and wise Temora that he
learns some of the deepest secrets.

All journeys must find an end. Argus leaves the fair
and travels on alone, until his last and greatest
adventure beckons him home. There he tells, for the
approval of his elders, the seven stories which are
now his story. But all is not done.

There is one more chapter to be lived out in the story
of Argus.

'...an extraordinary story...I would commend it to
everybody. Although ostensibly it's a children's book
it's something that any adult can read with great
pleasure. It's one of those books that don't actually
belong to any particular age group...like *The Snow
Goose*'
Terry Lane, ABC RADIO

John Marsden
Out of Time

James reads by his open bedroom window at night.
Other lives and other worlds beckon. One of these
worlds is conjured by old Mr Woodford, a physicist
who looks more like an accountant and who constructs
a strange black box.

One day when James slips into the laboratory, he
makes a dreadful discovery and learns to master a
great power.

Who is the little boy in Mexico who scratches pictures
of aeroplanes in the dust? How will the girl caught in
a wartime bomb blast be reunited with her parents?
And why does James sit alone in his island of silence?

With *Out of Time* John Marsden has produced a novel
that will further enhance his reputation as one of the
most successful writers of fiction for teenagers. This is
a challenging novel which poses a new question on
every page as it draws us into an ever-widening series
of mysteries, into magical, dangerous worlds—in and
out of time.

John Marsden
Letters from the Inside

Dear Tracey
I don't know why I'm answering your ad, to be
honest. It's not like I'm into pen pals, but it's a boring
Sunday here, wet, everyone's out, and I thought it'd
be something different . . .

Dear Mandy
Thanks for writing. You write so well, much better
than me. I put the ad in for a joke, like a dare, and
yours was the only good answer . . .

Two teenage girls. An innocent beginning to friendship. Two complete strangers who get to know each
other a little better each time a letter is written and
answered.

Mandy has a dog with no name, an older sister, a
creepy brother, and some boy problems. Tracey has
a horse, two dogs and a cat, an older sister and
brother, and a great boyfriend. They both have hopes
and fears . . . and secrets.

'John Marsden's *Letters from the Inside* is, in a word,
unforgettable. But this epistolary novel deserves
more than one word. It is absolutely shattering as it
brings to vivid life two teenage girls and then
strangles your heart over what happens to their
relationship . . . John Marsden is a major writer who
deserves world-wide acclaim'
ROBERT CORMIER

John Marsden
Checkers

She has parents, a brother, friends and a dog.

Sometimes the dog seems like the only one she can trust.

Her life is about to fall apart.

The dog is Checkers.

The book is unforgettable.

Praise for *Checkers*:

'…a terribly moving book…a subject that hasn't been written about much in children's literature…for anyone from ages fourteen to eighty-five'
BOOKSHOW

'…shattering…'
WEST AUSTRALIAN

'…intense…'
SUNDAY AGE

'…a wonderful story teller…'
GOLD COAST BULLETIN

'…heart-wrenching…'
HERALD SUN

John Marsden
Dear Miffy

'You can squeeze my lemon, baby, juice runs down my legs.'

Sex, I can't stop thinking about it, but. It's like the best sweetest torture ever invented. It tears you apart but you wouldn't want it any other way. It's the drug you never try to give up . . .

Tony writes letters.

To Miffy.

And breaks your heart.

Is there something wrong when your main ambition in life is to be dead?

'. . . Marsden can be relied upon to capture the imagination of several generations simultaneously'
HERALD SUN

'Marsden jerks you out of your comfort zone, confronting you with the realities of life, demanding you sit up and take notice. A fantastic read for young adults and adults alike'
QUEENSLAND TIMES

Learn great new writing skills, with John Marsden

You are invited to spend a few days with John Marsden at one of Australia's most beautiful properties.

The Tye Estate is just 25 minutes from Melbourne's Tullamarine Airport, and is perfectly set up for writing camps and other activities.

Every school holidays, John takes writing and drama camps, where you can improve your skills, make new friends, expand your thinking, and have a huge heap of fun.

Accommodation is modern and comfortable; meals are far removed from the shepherd's pie they gave you at your last school camp, and supervision is by friendly and experienced staff.

Between the workshops with John, you can explore 850 acres of spectacular bush, looking out for rare and highly endangered species like Tiger Quolls and Powerful Owls, as well as koalas, platypuses, wedgetail eagles, kangaroos and wallabies.

Mountain bikes, bushwalking, orienteering, and a picnic at nearby Hanging Rock, are among the highlights of your memorable stay at the Tye Estate.

School groups in term time are also welcome.

For details, write to:

The Tye Estate
RMB 1250
ROMSEY
VICTORIA 3434

Or fax: (61) 03 54 270395
Phone: (61) 03 54 270384